Forever Fat

Forever Fat

Essays by the Godfather

Lee Gutkind

UNIVERSITY OF NEBRASKA PRESS
LINCOLN AND LONDON

Acknowledgments for the use of previously
published material appear on page 179.

∞

Library of Congress Cataloging-in-Publication Data
Gutkind, Lee.
Forever fat: essays by the Godfather / Lee Gutkind.
p.   cm.
ISBN 0-8032-2194-0 (cloth: alk. paper)
1. Gutkind, Lee.   2. Authors, American—20th
century—Biography.   3. College teachers—United States—
Biography.   4. Editors—United States—Biography.
5. Creative writing (Higher education)   6. Creative
nonfiction (Urbana, Ill.)   7. Prose literature—Technique.
8. Nonfiction novel—Technique.   I. Title.
PS3557.U88Z464   2003
808'.0092—dc21
2002073292

To my parents,
To God,
To Squirrel Hill,
To Mr. Meyers,
To Irene, wherever you are,
And to James Wolcott

Contents

Acknowledgments   ix

An Introduction: Becoming the Godfather   xi

Who . . . What . . . Is Crazy?   1

Forever Fat   20

A History of My Father   42

Mr. Meyers   52

Teeth   57

Dog Story   68

Clarity   74

Waiting Away   92

Charlie Looks Good   99

Desperately Seeking Irene   113

Low-Clearance Story   132

WWMG   146

Intimate Details   171

Source Acknowledgments   179

Acknowledgments

There are people to thank: my agent, Andrew Blauner; Ladette Randolph; Elizabeth Hodges, who read an early draft; Sheila May Stein, who read a later draft; Judith Kitchen for her wise counsel; and my faithful second ex-wife, Patricia Park, who read and responded to every draft I wrote over a relentless five-year period.

An Introduction

Becoming the Godfather

What is it about creative nonfiction that makes people want to attack or make unfunny jokes about it—or about anyone having any connection with it? Over the past ten years, I have discussed the genre and the meaning of the term at colleges and universities and conferences in the United States, Europe, and Australia. But wherever I go there are the inevitable questions and complaints, especially about that first word—*creative*—which insults academics and scares journalists to death. "Why can't our work be creative, too?" they whine. Why are their essays on Milton or postmodernism or their articles concerning the local water authority considered criticism and reportage, respectively, while my prose about cross-country motorcycling or the medical world is considered artistic and literary?

People sometimes become so indignant that they entangle the terms they want to attack, confusing, for example, "creative nonfiction" with "noncreative fiction" or talking with great intensity about the "nonfiction essay"—as though there's an alternative. Those who are especially clever will observe that "creative nonfiction" is an oxymoron. Some will realize that "nonfiction" is also an oxymoron. A couple of months ago a woman who spotted me at Ronald Reagan Washington National Airport began pointing and yelling, "Hey, it's the uncreative fiction guy!"

The fact that I was recognized by a total stranger in a city hundreds of miles from where I live stems from a four-page feature article in *Vanity Fair*, "Me, Myself and I," by James Wolcott, who had snide and nasty observations about the term "creative nonfiction"—and about me. Wolcott boiled all creative nonfiction down to what he called "confessional writing" and took to task as "navel gazers" nearly any writer who had been the least bit self-revelatory in his or her work. ("Never have so many [writers] shared so much of so little; no personal detail is too mundane to share.") His definition of creative nonfiction? A "sickly transfusion, whereby the weakling personal voice of sensitive fiction is inserted into the beery carcass of nonfiction . . . to form a big, earnest blob of me-first sensibility." Inexplicably Wolcott zeroed in on the memoir and made it seem as though that was creative nonfiction in its totality, while ignoring the significant information-oriented work done by John McPhee, Annie Dillard, Tracy Kidder, Gay Talese, and many others.

Wolcott reserved an especially interesting title and role for me as "the godfather behind creative nonfiction." He abhorred the fact that I travel and talk about creative nonfiction all over the world (he called me a "human octopus"), write books about creative nonfiction, publish a journal (*Creative Nonfiction*), direct a creative nonfiction writers' conference, edit a series of books for new writers in creative nonfiction, and teach creative nonfiction in a creative writing program, which, he maintained, collectively ruined the audience for fiction. Because of the proliferation of these courses, "the short story has become a minor arts and craftsy skill, like Indian pottery," he stated.

It was unfortunate that Wolcott had so much to say in such a major publication concerning a subject about which he knew so little. (He had never been involved in a creative writing program or taken a writing course.) In truth creative writing programs have actually legitimized creative or "literary" nonfiction—making it more important in the literary world than ever before by acknowledging, albeit belatedly, the awesome challenge and intrinsic art of the genre and indirectly affecting, in a very positive way, *Vanity Fair* and Wolcott himself. Without the new appreciation for (creative) nonfiction as an art form as significant as fiction and poetry, Wolcott's opinions would be less important, while magazines like *Vanity Fair*, GQ, *Harper's*, *Esquire*, and others might not attract the advertising and wield the influence that enhances profits and prominence.

When I started teaching in the English department at the University of Pittsburgh in the early 1970s, the concept of an "artful" or "literary" nonfiction was considered unlikely, to say the least. My colleagues snickered when I proposed teaching a creative nonfiction course, while the dean of the College of Arts and Sciences proclaimed that nonfiction in general—forget the use of the word *creative*—was at its best a craft, not too different from plumbing. As the chairman of our department put it one day in a faculty meeting while we were debating the legitimacy of the course: "After all, gentlemen (the fact that many of his colleagues were women often slipped his mind), we're interested in literature here—not writing." That remark and the subsequent debate had been precipitated by a contingent of students from the school newspaper who marched on the chairman's office and politely requested more nonfiction writing courses—"of the creative kind."

One colleague, aghast at the prospect of this "new thing" (creative nonfiction), carried a dozen of his favorite books to the meeting—poetry, fiction, and nonfiction—gave a belabored mini-review of each, and then, pointing a finger at the editor of the paper and pounding a fist, stated: "After you read all these books and understand what they mean, I will consider voting for a course called creative nonfiction. Otherwise, I don't want to be bothered." Luckily most of my colleagues didn't want to be bothered fighting the school newspaper, so the course was approved—and I become one of the first people, if not the first, to teach creative nonfiction on a university level, anywhere. This was 1973.

Since then, creative nonfiction courses in creative writing programs have grown steadily on graduate and undergraduate levels. Being awarded tenure in the English department at Pittsburgh in 1979 was another milestone—perhaps another first for literary nonfiction. Now there are many tenure-track professorial positions for writers whose specialty is nonfiction, exclusively. This was no small feat. The practice in English departments and writing programs then was to appoint writers who had "legitimized" themselves by becoming accomplished in fiction or poetry—a recognizable literary art—but who could also stretch and teach nonfiction, an ancillary skill. As the job market tightened in the early 1980s and a few nonfiction positions were posted, an amazing transition occurred: Poets, short-story writers and composition Ph.D.'s who had written articles for newspapers and semi-scholarly journals in their younger days and who had previously concealed or ignored their journalistic backgrounds, however slight, were suddenly reinventing themselves as creative nonfiction writers.

Some very accomplished poets and fiction writers were taking nonfiction more seriously, however, by actually practicing what others were pretending. John Updike published his first collection of essays, *Assorted Prose*. Diane Ackerman began involving herself in the natural world and writing spellbinding articles for the *New Yorker*, while W. S. Merwin's first memoir, *Unframed Originals*, became a best seller. Prominent writers crossing genres and adding their talent and prestige to nonfiction was a significant part of the process of legitimizing creative nonfiction as an entity beyond journalism and on the same general level as fiction and poetry.

Vanity Fair wasn't alone in attacking the genre in the late 1990s, however. The *New York Times*, the *New Yorker*, and other major newspapers and magazines made it clear that even though they recognized an explosion in the nonfiction form (mostly memoir) they also predicted a quick demise. And by the way, they hated the term "creative nonfiction," preferring narrative nonfiction, literary journalism, or expository writing, among others. In its precious and traditional simplicity, the *New Yorker* called the creative nonfiction it published by John McPhee, Roger Angell, Jane Kramer and others, "fact pieces." Even today, bookstores and libraries choose either to stack creative nonfiction under "essays" or matched up with subject matter. Thus John McPhee's *Basin and Range* and Annie Dillard's *Pilgrim at Tinker Creek* along with Tracy Kidder's *Soul of a New Machine*, nonfiction Pulitzer Prize recipients, will be marginalized to science and nature or technology, respectively. Anything but "literature," where most poetry and fiction are shelved, let alone "creative nonfiction."

What does it mean to be creative? And what is so difficult or terrible to contemplate about the term? Why is it bad to acknowledge that you are trying, as a writer, to show imagination and to demonstrate artistic or intellectual inventiveness? Nonfiction writers aren't boasting or bragging by utilizing the word in describing what we do—and it is not a concept that others or I have coined out of the air. Creative nonfiction—writing nonfiction using literary techniques like scene, dialogue, description, while allowing the personal point of view and voice (reflection) rather than maintaining the sham of objectivity—is hardly a new idea. Hunter S. Thompson (*Hell's Angels*), Gay Talese (*Fame and Obscurity*), Norman Mailer (*Armies of the Night*), and Tom Wolfe (*The Electric Kool-Aid Acid Test*) were introducing literary techniques and personal voice into their nonfiction work in the 1960s—a style then called the "new journalism." Earlier work by Lillian Ross—and much earlier by George Orwell—are clearly situated under the creative nonfiction umbrella.

The term was eventually adopted by the National Endowment for the Arts to represent the different styles within the genre (memoir, immersion journalism, and so on), an "official" acknowledgment of the distinction between the way in which the literary or creative essay is written compared to the traditional essay or news report. This difference has to do with storytelling—employing real life experiences of the writer or people they know or people they learn about through the techniques of immersion or involvement in a dramatic, often suspenseful, sequence—in order to communicate information or establish a special meaning or idea. Creative nonfiction is different because writers aren't constrained by traditional academic or journalistic straitjackets. Literally or symbolically, we can dye our hair green, wear earrings in our navels, and allow our own personalities to appear on the page with our ideas and observations—a seemingly special violation to the journalist, who has been locked into the inverted pyramid 5W format (who-what-when-where-why) over the past half-century and beyond.

I am not disputing the overabundance of "navel gazers," as Wolcott put it—writers who are primarily inward and self obsessed—or the notion that there hasn't been an overemphasized craze for this sort of personal (sometimes too personal) writing as of late. But there's also an explosion of altogether brilliant nonfiction prose being written today by people who can reveal their feelings or the feelings of the people about whom they are writing while communicating compelling information and striking some sort of universal chord. What about *Angela's Ashes* (Frank McCourt), *A Natural History of the Senses* (Diane Ackerman), *Autobiography of a Face* (Lucy Grealy), *The Professor and the Madman* (Simon Winchester), *Brothers and Keepers* (John Edgar Wideman), to name a few?

Journalists have, over the years, been so stifled from being creative that they don't exactly understand what the word creative might signify beyond the parameters of fiction. William Zinsser, author of the highly respected text *On Writing Well*, has acknowledged his uneasiness with the phrase "creative nonfiction" because he associated "creative" either with fiction or with writers who "fudge the truth." Young writers, he fears, will take the word creative as a license to fabricate. Zinsser agrees that nonfiction can be creative when "a writer raises the craft to an art by imposing an interesting shape or organizing idea on it," which to me is one of many ways in which writers can write with style without sacrificing substance. But clearly he doesn't have much confidence in the intelligence of our young people, if he thinks that students will take creativity as a license to lie.

In the past couple of years, a number of journalists have been discovered and disgraced for, literally, fudging the truth. In 1997, Stephen Glass admitted to fabricating parts of twenty-seven articles for the *New Republic*, where he worked as a reporter, and for the *New York Times*, *George*, and *Harper's*. He even provided fake supporting material, including self-created web sites, to outfox his fact checkers. And a columnist for the *Boston Globe*, Patricia Smith, a Pulitzer Prize finalist, admitted to fabricating the people and the quotations in four of her columns in 1999. In one case she made up an entire column about a woman dying of cancer. These reporters, only two examples among many, weren't claiming that they were trying to be creative; they took liberties that were blatantly dishonest. The journalism community must learn to police themselves more carefully—rather than fantasize about the potential damage that can be done in other glass houses.

Unfortunately, however, with so many new people discovering creative nonfiction from so many different orientations (especially in the areas of psychology, literature, and composition), the journalistic, fact-oriented roots of creative nonfiction are often forgotten—or ignored. Writers can become too enamored with the creative part of the term, paying precious little homage to the nonfiction part. There must be a delicate balance between style and substance. Whether writing memoir or dramatic reportage, creative nonfiction writers must always work as hard as necessary to be true to the facts; there are some creative nonfiction writers who don't care about accuracy or consider it unimportant. These writers lose credibility when they are writing nonfiction and not paying attention to verifiable information.

I recently participated in a panel at a writers' conference in which one woman, writing about a town in Germany during the Nazi era, stated that she wouldn't employ the name of the town because she was keeping her options open just in case she wanted to change what she was doing to fiction. What is that all about, one wonders? If she doesn't know whether she's writing fiction or nonfiction—then she is writing fiction. Readers don't appreciate or deserve such sleight of hand.

John Berendt, author of the best selling *Midnight in the Garden of Good and Evil*, admitted to making up saucy dialogue for a real-life character and creating situations in order to more easily manipulate his narrative. "I call it 'rounding the corners,'" he explained, adding that he has no regrets because, by doing this, he feels he is giving his readers "a better story." But it is not a true story and it denotes inexcusable laziness. When confronted with a character who might not have exactly scintillating things to say, a good writer, rather than making up better stuff, will work harder to discover other aspects of the subject that are interesting, like talking to other people about the character in question—or make better connections between one part of an essay to another, or simply work on getting the character to reveal themselves—rather than resorting to fiction.

At the same time, while facts can be checked and confirmed, not all truth is verifiable. This is especially important to acknowledge for those writing memoir. Ideas and feelings fished out of a person or unearthed from memory can't often be fact-checked. Scenes, which are recreated, conversations that have been recalled and recounted from the distant past, will be highly personal and subjective. But in creative nonfiction we draw the line; we do not make up information of any kind—for any reason. We do our best to replicate with truth and accuracy exactly what we believe has happened, even if, in the real world, there is a possibility that it hasn't happened in exactly the way we describe it or that other people will disagree with our interpretations.

This is not a new idea, historically, but many journalists have become so cemented into the traditional 5w form of reporting that they are often afraid or unable to try anything different—afraid that they simply don't have the talent or the energy to write and report in a creative manner. The timidity of their editors and the narrow range of their literary perspective have devastated their potential as serious writers. Many of the newspaper reporters who enroll in my M.F.A. (Masters of Fine Arts in Creative Writing) classes experience great difficulty writing longer essays—twelve pages, three thousand words, focusing on one theme. Intellectual investigation is an unmined concept in daily journalism. Reporters have been trained for so long to write short pieces, to dumb-down their ideas to a sixth grade level—and to think in quotes and sound bites—that they can't introduce real characters with intelligent perceptions. It is ironic that journalists like to refer to what they are doing as a "story"—but they aren't stories; rather they are reports, with a few scenic elements sometimes included by those willing to devote an extra effort.

Which is not to say that the journalistic community hasn't recognized the inevitable shift to a more creative concept of journalism; they are simply not talking about it. For two years, I mentored reporters and editors on the science desk at National Public Radio (NPR), teaching a style of journalism in which story or narrative is given much more attention, without a loss in substance, integrity, or verifiable facts. Up to this point, most journalists have maintained that a concentration on story (style) endangers the journalistic integrity of the final product—which is a legitimate concern if the reporter devotes the same amount of time and effort to style and story as would occur in his or her traditional work. The problem is that most journalists devote most of their efforts to the information-gathering process. Then they sit down and write their "story," basically relying on their skills as writers to be clear, concise, and compelling. It's good when a natural narrative emerges—but not unusual when it doesn't.

By enlisting my help, NPR's science reporters, editors, and producers have symbolically and literally endorsed their commitment to the story form. They are authorizing and encouraging reporters to invest extra time and effort to understand and integrate a dramatic, suspenseful, compelling story structure into the reports they file. NPR hasn't backed away from the term "creative nonfiction," while, ironically, the *New York Times*, while pretending that creative nonfiction doesn't exist, has endorsed and adopted, in an all-encompassing way, virtually every idea that creative nonfiction stands for.

Front-page news is now often told in a story-oriented fashion in the *Times*. Here's the beginning of just one story, selected at random, from its twelve-part series, "How Race Is Lived in America," but you can find such examples on any day of the week: "It must have been 1 o'clock. That's when the white man usually comes out of this glass office and stands on the scaffolding above the factory floor. He stood with his palms on the rails, his elbows out. He looked like a tower guard up there or a border patrol agent. He stood with his head cocked."

Here we have specificity of description and intimacy of detail, written in the cold staccato rhythm of the poet, while a character has been created and an inner point of view (the reader sees the world through the eyes of the character) is established. A few sentences later, the conflict telegraphed in this paragraph is launched: "The white man stood and watched for the next two hours as the blacks worked in their group and the Mexicans in theirs.... At shift change, the black man walked away, hosed himself down and turned in his knives. Then he let go. He threatened to murder the boss. He promised to quit. He said he was losing his mind, which made for good comedy since he was standing near a conveyor chain of severed hogs' heads, their mouths yoked open. 'Who that cracker think he is?' the black man wanted to know. There were enough hogs, he said, 'not to worry about no fleck of meat being left on the bone. Keep treating me like a Mexican and I'll beat him.' "

So here we have the other anchors of creative nonfiction—dramatic, compelling story energized by electrifying dialogue. Call it what you want, but it is the epitome of creative nonfiction.

It is particularly interesting that creative nonfiction has experienced such an amazing renaissance in the past decade, especially in the memoir category, toward which James Wolcott chose to direct the most vituperative of his comments. Memoirists, writers who have accelerated the pulse, expanded the barriers, increased the dimensions of the previously more confining and traditional publishing world, have become characters journalists love to lambaste— also completely without authority. Creative nonfiction writers are "out there," highly visible, sometimes obnoxiously so, walking the line between truth and reality, style and substance, memory and imagination. So we can make people, especially those traditionalists anchored in the past, feel resentful and angry, as in the case of James Wolcott. We can and often do handcuff emotions to manipulate feelings, not subtly like the poet, but in a very obvious and titillating way.

In this regard I am thinking of Lucy Grealy's poetic and powerful self-deprecation in *Autobiography of a Face* and Kathryn Harrison's humiliating confessions of sleeping with her Presbyterian-minister father in *The Kiss*. These writers are walking the edge, testing literary and societal norms and, for good and for bad, creating excitement and controversy. I don't condone the liberties of writers anxious to excoriate themselves for personal gain. But I appreciate the spirit of their revelations, their willingness to test boundaries rather than sitting comfortably in the safe spaces of respectability, whining about their lack of prominence, criticizing others who have daringly ventured forth with new ideas and concepts. I would not do what Edmund Morris did in creating a fictional Ronald Reagan (*Dutch*) to illuminate the dead fish of the man he was struggling to capture, but I admire his resourcefulness. He created unprecedented interest and stimulated intellectual discourse about a man people revered, but knew nothing about. He also made a lot of money.

In its purest form, creative nonfiction is, similarly, nothing else but real—with all of the potential flaws and warts of any real human being. Mostly people attack writers of creative nonfiction because we are too difficult and complicated to figure out. And we can become much too embarrassingly public. We don't fit into the traditional form of reportage. But how can you apply the 5w formula to the revelations of the Clinton era, the O. J. Simpson media circus, or the disclosures of the Enron scandal? Who would want to? That's not the inherent challenge of literature—minimizing larger-than-life characters and their stories for the sake of brevity and space. Journalists have difficulty thinking in more than twelve column inches—a narrow format for an outsized subject. Creative nonfiction writers visualize a world in three multicolored, multi-conflicting dimensions.

In a subsequent interview in the *Chronicle of Higher Education*, James Wolcott said that he had learned most of what he had picked up about writing while working in the classified-ad section of the *Village Voice* rather than by studying in a creative writing program, and that today all of these writing programs are producing creative writers who are "coddled and swaddled" and who would never get jobs. I am not certain that he is wrong about the value of creative writing programs, which I think are ill-suited for many of the students who support them. But his attitude in the face of ignorance is indicative of the two-dimensional surface-skimming orientation inherent in magazine and newspaper journalism.

Wolcott also told an interviewer that he was "distrustful of memory," which is why he would never write a memoir. (He subsequently published a novel.) But perhaps he and others who are so critical of creative nonfiction are more distrustful of what they might, in fact, remember when they actually started to search their souls and think about their lives with an open and analytic perspective. This is a frightening concept to people unable to face or reveal their innermost feelings—or who just don't recognize the value or understand the method in doing so.

That, in fact, is the essence and the meaning of creative nonfiction: the ability to capture the personal and the private and to make it mean something significant to a larger audience and to provide intellectual substance that will affect readers—perhaps even incite them to action or to change their thinking—in a compelling and unforgettable way.

My thinking was changed by my experience with Wolcott and *Vanity Fair*—incidentally—in a way that James Wolcott might not find great pleasure in discovering. For weeks after "Me, Myself and I" was published, our subscription inquiries at *Creative Nonfiction* shot up; we got phone calls from Hollywood producers, seeking new stories for their movie mills. People were recognizing me in airports, restaurants—and congratulating me. Although Wolcott's attack caught me by surprise and might be described as mean-spirited, I believe, in retrospect, that the attention he generated and the controversy it triggered actually fortified the cause and elevated the discourse surrounding high-quality creative nonfiction literature, which is why it is important to remember it now.

In the end, I discovered the truth in Oscar Wilde's observation, more than a century ago, found in the first chapter of *The Picture of Dorian Gray*: "There is only one thing in the world worse than being talked about, and that is not being talked about." And I have James Wolcott to thank for it.

Who . . . What . . . Is Crazy?

When I drove up to the house, Daniel was walking toward me. I got out of the car and waited for him to approach. Even though he waved and flashed a quick smile, he seemed grim and befuddled. "What's wrong, Dan?"

Daniel had been working at a rental property I owned, cleaning out the basement, a filthy job he savored. Nothing made Daniel happier than getting dirty, especially with a bunch of junk. Daniel had rummaged through trash for as long as I had known him, rescuing an array of worthless mechanical objects—manual typewriters, speedometers, radios, lamps, rusty tools, old motors. Keys of any size, type, or condition were his passion, as were locks, whether or not they corresponded to the keys. Sometimes he managed to clean or fix a derelict item of junk and sell it at a Sunday flea market, but usually Daniel was more interested in contemplating these items in the questionable safety of his room.

When I put my hands on his shoulders, Daniel immediately began to whine like a frightened child. Tears were streaming down his face. "A man molested me." He reached down and began squeezing his buttocks. "Oh, it hurts," he wailed. "It hurts so bad back there."

I walked him over to the steps leading to the house and sat him down on the stoop, uncertain how to respond. Ruffling his curly hair with my hand, I joked about how dirty he was and made a crack about his ears, which were unusually small. I could almost always get him to laugh by poking fun at his ears and pointing out that he was most handsome on Halloween when he wore a mask. In truth, Daniel was kind of weird looking. His head was small, like his ears, and he was short, but very heavy. When I met him he was twelve; he had been slender, a feather of a boy. But an interest in weight lifting, combined with a voracious appetite for starchy foods and secret doses of steroids, had bloated him considerably.

Daniel poured out his story. He had worked in the basement for a half-hour or so, dragging out a mess of discarded timber, empty paint cans, and old furniture, then decided to take a five-minute walk to a nearby convenience store for a soda. There's a bank of pay phones on the corner beside the store, and as he was passing, a phone was ringing. Daniel answered. A male voice at the other end said he was waiting for Daniel and that he would kill him if he didn't do exactly what he was told. Suddenly, a car screeched to a halt at the curb. A man, unshaven, dressed in black trousers, black shirt, and black patent-leather shoes and waving a knife, ordered Daniel inside. Daniel complied. They drove across a corner, down a side street, and into an alley, whereupon the man led Daniel through a clump of bushes behind an abandoned building. Following orders, Daniel kissed the man on the lips, then, under threat of the knife, sank to his knees and performed oral sex. Finally, Daniel lay face down on the ground. He felt a sharp and intrusive pain. The man entered him. Now Daniel was nearly hysterical. "He said he'd kill me if I told anyone. What am I going to do?"

I could not answer his question, for I felt dumbfounded and conflicted. This incident had occurred in my neighborhood, an area in which I lived with my son, considered the safest in the city. Not that crime never occurred here, but such a brazen incident in the middle of a bright and busy Saturday afternoon was unlikely. Besides, there was Daniel's history to consider, beginning with the abuse and neglect that led authorities to permanently separate Daniel from his family when he was ten years old.

As Daniel's parent surrogate or "big brother," I knew that the abuse he suffered during his early years had been documented and resulted in posttraumatic stress disorder (PTSD), wherein earlier trauma is reenacted in flashbacks. This may have accounted for the new and questionable incidents of violence and molestation he had reported. Only a couple of weeks ago, Daniel had come home with his face bruised and his books and wallet missing. He claimed to have been attacked by four black kids, wielding pipes, who stole his money and beat him up. Later, witnesses reported that he had actually gotten into a fight with a neighborhood kid, who was white—and lost. Last year, Daniel told of being followed by a bearded man who had forced him into a Cadillac and molested him.

Daniel's recent credibility was especially suspect. Hadn't he, one Saturday afternoon, removed all the manhole covers from the sewer system on the periphery of his group home and covered the holes with twigs, grass, and weeds as "booby traps"? Hadn't he promised, after I explained the danger, to immediately replace the manhole covers and hadn't he reneged on that promise? Didn't he lie frequently about where he went and what he did, using his learning disabilities and the side effects from antidepressant medication as justifications for forgetting and making mistakes? The booby trap incident had been especially disturbing because it made me realize that Daniel's defensiveness could distort his sense of right and wrong. The social worker assigned to his case observed that Daniel had been so thoroughly battered by his family and the child welfare system that "rescued" him that it was impossible for him to feel compassion. The fact that someone could have been hurt—or killed—by his booby traps meant little or nothing to Daniel, who frequently declared, "I don't care about anyone else."

But I knew another side of him. Daniel was an isolated innocent. He read at a second-grade level and, living with alcoholic parents in a rooming house or in mental health institutions most of his life, he had existed like a primitive in the jungle—separated from the outside world. Even the adults at the group home where he now lived, or the special school he attended, hardly ever talked with him about anything other than fast food and television—to the point where he could not distinguish between the story programs and the news. He believed that Michael Knight (of the *Knight Rider* TV show) was real and that McDonald's had invented hamburgers. Every conversation I had with him, especially when we first met, became endlessly convoluted because, no matter what he asked, I had to backtrack to the beginning to put my answer into perspective.

I once told him I was going out of town, flying. He said he had never been on an airplane. "How long does it take to fly on an airplane?"

"It depends on where you want to go. Now, I am going to New York. You know about New York? Grand Central Station? Times Square?" There was no recognition. He had never heard of New York.

"How much does it cost to ride in an airplane?"

"Well, where would you like to go?" He looked at me blankly. "Would you like to go to California?" He just looked at me.

"Dan, do you know about the oceans?"

"What's 'oceans'?"

"You know that there are different oceans on either side of the country?"

"No."

"The Atlantic and Pacific. If you fly to California, you'll be at the Pacific Ocean, and if you fly to Florida, you'll be at the Atlantic Ocean."

"How much does it cost to fly to Florida?"

"If you go one way, it will cost you one price, but if you go round trip, you'll get a discount."

"What's round trip?"

"It's when you go both ways."

"Well," said Daniel, "what's discount?"

Daniel continued to whimper as I tried to decide how to proceed. At the very least, I had to get him away from this house and the fear that the mysterious man, whether real or imagined, was going to come back for him. Daniel was confused about his sexual orientation. I remembered a story he told me of another unshaven man who lived in the woods across from his home who would periodically sneak into the room he occupied with his sister—and molest them both. At the time we talked about this incident, he asked me, "Does this mean I'm gay?"

"It means that the person who raped you was evil or crazy, or both. It has nothing to do with you," I told him, although we both knew that I was not being accurate. Whatever had happened to Daniel was directly related to his curiosity about sex or his willingness to become victimized for the sake of drama and his need for attention. Hurriedly, we gathered his possessions and climbed into my car.

I drove in the general direction of the convenience store until Daniel pointed to the street to which the man had taken him. I turned the corner, Daniel directing me into the alley he had described. For the first time I began to believe that the incident could have happened. The alleyway was not dark or narrow, but it was clearly out of the way, as was the building to which he pointed, set off in a secluded corner of a vacant lot. The underbrush around the building was thick and concealing. If molestation had occurred, it could have happened here. As I sat in the car and contemplated his story from this perspective, I could hear the distant clatter of an approaching helicopter. This site is very close to a local hospital, known for its cutting-edge trauma and emergency care facilities. Patients were transported into the area via ambulance or to a rooftop heliport day and night. Sitting in this isolated and self-contained little spot in the middle of my neighborhood and listening to the sound of the whirling rotor, now clopping directly above our heads, was a familiar and oddly comforting refrain from the distant past.

When I was seven years old, my pregnant mother went to the hospital. Her return, one week later, to our tiny two-bedroom, second-floor apartment, with my infant twin brothers, Michael and Richard, forever changed my life.

The morning of their arrival, I stood in the hallway on the top of the stairs and watched the deliverymen carry up the cribs with the wooden jailhouse bars and situate them in my bedroom, side by side. The hallway led to the kitchen on one side, my parents' bedroom on the other side and my bedroom adjacent to my parents. The doorway to the living room was behind me.

Only after the deliverymen left the house, did I realize something had happened that I had not anticipated. I knew I was gaining brothers, but it never occurred to me, until that very moment, that I would lose my personal space.

The bedroom had been my escape from a seething volcano named Jack. Any conceivable misstep from his first born son—a disrespectful comment, a forgotten chore—could trigger my father's sudden eruption.

Blood rushing to his cheeks, infusing his face with redness. The leather belt slips from the waistband of his trousers and appears in his hand, folded in half, tip against buckle. He stalks me. Usually, a dozen wild, haphazard strokes . . . in the butt, on my face or ears . . . wherever.

When his temper erupted, I would escape into my room. Sometimes he would pursue me, but eventually he would leave me alone. Thank God for my room. I was like an animal in its den licking its wounds. Safe for the moment, but forever on guard.

Now I no longer owned that space.

From that point onward, I waited each night in the hallway at the top of these stairs, reading, listening to the radio—activities forbidden in my room for fear of disturbing my brothers—until I heard the key in the latch of the front door.

My father home from work. I feel his body leaning into the first few steps, hear his shoes scrape each stair, as I dash into my room and leap into bed.

He pauses at the top of the stairs. I lay frozen on my sheets under the tent of my covers.

Would he, after a long day, hang up his coat, turn to the left and go into the kitchen for dinner? Go to his right to his bedroom to change into comfortable clothing? Or walk to my door in between and push it open?

Sometimes he paused at the top of the stairs. There was a conversation with my mother. I could only make out a scattering of words. My mother was volunteering details about my poor behavior. Caught in the middle, trying to balance the demands of the two men in her life, her sympathies and motivations were ambiguous.

Footsteps. The door opening. Will he yell? Will he say, "I know you aren't sleeping; I know what you did today," then charge my bed and pummel me awake? Or, will he decide to let it go—"temporarily"?

If "temporarily," I have hope.

I will stay in bed until he finishes his shower the following morning and goes into his bedroom to dress. I will run into the bathroom, relieve myself, brush my teeth and rush back to my room before he finishes. I will dress while he eats breakfast. I will appear in the kitchen when he is in a hurry to go to work. Not much time now to punish me. "Wait until tonight," he says. The fear never ends.

To get through my sleepless nights without waking my brothers and thereby making my father angry, I made up a number of bizarre, imaginary games, many of which were sporting events. I set my wastebasket on top of my chest of drawers, tied my socks into knots, and shot baskets. I sneaked down to the basement in my pajamas and golfed rolls of toilet paper through the coalbin door with a broomstick. I wedged my pillow upright against the wall in the corner of my bed and boxed it for the heavyweight championship of the world.

Some of the games included a boy in school, Marc Lindenbaum. I had known Marc all of my life. He and I were the same age. His birthday was Halloween, and my mother and his mother, Doris, and a few other ladies played poker together each Thursday night. When it was time for "the girls," (how these ladies always referred to themselves) to come to our house, my father would usually go out to dinner. With my mother and her friends talking and laughing and clicking their plastic poker chips on the table in the kitchen, they paid me little attention. Lots of times I would leave the bedroom and creep up the hallway, commando-style on my stomach, to listen to their gossip and entertain myself.

Usually, I slithered under the table with a pencil and a tablet and diagramed the varicose veins in the women's legs. In my bedroom the following day, I would put my toy cars on the lines I had drawn, which copied the varicose designs on their legs, and pretending they were highways of love, follow them upward from the calf, over the knee, along the thigh and then gun my engines and squeal my tires in a mad dash toward the sacred jungle area—a place I called "Joy City." I don't know if the women were clued into what I was doing with their varicose veins under their poker table, but I was often able to remain quiet and unobtrusive long enough so that they forgot I was around.

Which is how I learned that Marc Lindenbaum was sick and dying. I was only eleven or twelve when I overheard Doris Lindenbaum discuss the doctors' reports alluding to Marc's declining health.

"I thought the last operation cut out the malignancy," my mother said.

"We thought that the surgery would stop the growth, but it didn't work. It was a chance. The poor kid, he doesn't know."

"He doesn't know anything?"

"He knows something is wrong," said Mrs. Lindenbaum, "but not that he has cancer."

Cancer, I knew from Miss Schlegel's science class, fifth period of the fourth grade, was something that grew and grew in your body. *Malignancy* was a word I was unfamiliar with, but clearly it was something nobody wanted.

I saw Lindenbaum walking to school the following morning. Lindenbaum bounced when he walked, as if he had shoes with springs for soles, he went up so high with each step, and I wondered how a person so close to death could look so happy. There was a chance that his mother was exaggerating or mistaken about Marc's upcoming death, but older people hardly ever joked about death because they were so close to it themselves. If his parents and my parents were convinced that Marc was going to die, then there could be no doubt. Marc had had it. I wondered if he was aware of his fate. Could Marc feel his blood turning to water, his heart beating slower, his brain ceasing to function, grinding to a halt like an unlubricated machine? "Soon I won't be around anymore," my grandparents, aunts, and uncles would sometimes say. Or, "I'm coming to the end of the line. My time is almost up." And more often than not, they were right. As they grew older, my grandparents and relatives and their friends were dropping off at an alarming rate. Their main social activity seemed to be attending funerals, either as visitors or victims. Had Marc, I wondered, gotten the word that he was next?

Through the rest of the day, I followed Lindenbaum, watching him in classes, trailing him to the bathroom and water fountain, studying him carefully for telltale signs of death. After school, I followed him home. Delevan, Marc's street, was very narrow, with cars parked on both sides, leaving a single through lane for traffic. Like the street, the houses were small and narrow, yards cluttered with bushes, hoses, sprinklers, canvas swimming pools, and patches of frail, hungry flowers. After Marc went inside, I walked back and forth past the house a number of times. First, I walked by quickly, head bent, as if I was on an important errand. In a while, I passed again, casually now, on a leisurely stroll. The third time, I crossed to the other side of the street, got down on my hands and knees, and crawled from bush to bush until I was directly opposite the house on my stomach. No one was on the porch. Everything was quiet, but the door was open, and through the screen I could see a lounge chair, a table, a vase, a television flickering. I watched for a long time, waiting for someone to walk past the door or come outside to hose down the sidewalk or sit and rock on the glider. But nobody came; no movement, no sound. The gray paint on the house was faded and chipping. Underneath the outer layer of gray, I could make out a previous layer of gray paint. And underneath a second was surely a third and perhaps even a fourth layer of gray, as if the whole house had been put together, beams and all, with succeeding layers of gray paint.

For quite a while, I lay on the moist cool grass, my chin propped on my palm, staring across the street at Lindenbaum's house, picturing Marc inside. Suddenly, I detected the odor of cooking cabbage, wafting like poison gas onto the street. The cabbage odor wrapped around me, captured me, just like death would capture Marc Lindenbaum, and no matter how hard I tried, I was unable to purge the putrid, rancid smell that came with the cabbage. I ran down the street and around the corner. I held my nose. I sneezed and coughed. But just as there was no escape from the stink of cabbage, the shroud of death, I suddenly realized, would never release you. A person could not die and then get up the next day and walk to school. Dead was forever. I had gone to my grandfather's funeral and I had never seen my grandfather again. You never came back when you were dead. Dead was what was going to happen to Marc Lindenbaum, even though he was only twelve years old and looked perfectly healthy—no bald head, no hair growing out of his ears and nose like the old people had, no brown-blotched skin.

The one thing to do, I concluded, to help Marc Lindenbaum was to make the last days of his life truly memorable, which is why, bright and early the following day, I waited for him in front of the school and handed him a small package wrapped in aluminum foil. "Here," I said. "Take it."

"What is it?"

"It's a walkie-talkie."

"Are you kidding?" he said, peeking under the foil. "This is a package of Lucky Strike cigarettes. You better watch it, Gutkind. You better not get caught with cigarettes at school."

"That's what it is disguised to look like, but I am telling you what it really is—a make-believe walkie-talkie. There's a built-in aerial in there—and the wires are all invisible. I painted them with invisible ink."

"This is no walkie-talkie."

"Yes it is. I'll show you." With my thumb, I flicked an imaginary switch on the side of the package and made a clicking noise with my mouth. "First you activate it with this switch. The switch is invisible so that no one will know how to activate or deactivate, except for me, you, and Kiner." I was referring to Ralph Kiner, former home-run-hitting left fielder for the Pittsburgh Pirates. Kiner was no longer a Pittsburgh Pirate by then—his playing days were over—but I treasured his memory.

"What do you mean, Kiner? This is ridiculous. You can't talk with Kiner on this thing. You couldn't even talk with Kiner if it was a real walkie-talkie."

"That's what you think, but I've perfected this make-believe walkie-talkie in my laboratory."

"You see," said Lindenbaum. "Even you say it is make-believe."

"Just because it is make-believe, doesn't mean it doesn't work," I told him.

"This is stupid."

"Gutkind to Lindenbaum. Gutkind to Lindenbaum," I barked into the cigarette package with the aluminum foil around it.

"This is really stupid," Lindenbaum said again.

"Can you hear me?"

"Yes I can hear you, of course I can hear you."

"So then," I told him. "It works."

"But I can hear you without the walkie-talkie."

"How do you know you can?"

"Because I hear you all the time."

"You can't hear Kiner."

"I can't hear Kiner with the walkie-talkie, either."

"That's what Kiner said you'd say. Kiner said that as long as you think the walkie-talkies work, they will work. But once you doubt make-believe walkie-talkie magic, its power dies."

I wanted Lindenbaum to believe this because, at the time, trapped in the dark in the bedroom that was once my private refuge and was now my prison, periodically stalked by a raging father, my most important objective was to believe in the world I made up. To believe in make-believe. The real world was lonely, dark, and terrifying—and my privacy had been stolen from me by the invasion of my brothers. Reaching out to Lindenbaum or Kiner through my make-believe walkie-talkie provided an outlet of relief for my fear, loneliness, and anxiety.

In bed at night holding the walkie-talkie in my hand, clicking the invisible switch and hearing the walkie-talkie crackle to life, feeling its warmth in my hands, I became the most popular person in my class. All the kids in school came to talk with me about their problems with parents or confusing moral dilemmas about watching girls take showers through holes in the shower-room walls at camp or fantasizing about breasts, those luscious nippled mounds of flesh and skin we called "bazoongies," or saying the word "fuck" out loud. I was their advisor. I held court. My assistant took numbers. Even parents and teachers came to discuss their students' and children's behaviors. Periodically, Ralph Kiner would call to praise my home-run-hitting ability. General Douglas MacArthur, using semaphore flags from his aircraft carrier headquarters, warned me of suspect Red Chinese infiltrations and asked me to investigate suspicious neighbors, purported to be members of the Communist Party. The walkie-talkies also provided me with an opportunity to vent my own frustrations with my first "shrink" figure, Marc Lindenbaum himself, expressing my worries about my angry, mean father, my constantly complaining mother, my crying brothers, who had invaded and seized my room and diverted all adult attention away from me. Through the walkie-talkie, Lindenbaum was my intimate confidant, whether he was willing to admit it or not.

"Please don't tell anyone what I said last night over the make-believe walkie-talkie," I often beseeched him the following morning.

"How can I tell anyone what you said over the make-believe walkie-talkie when I didn't hear you?"

"That's perfect! If anyone ever asks us, tell them the make-believe walkie-talkies don't exist."

The day I fight back.

The top of the stairway.

My father is whaling me with his leather belt.

I fled down the steps; he caught me on the landing and dragged me up to the top. We struggled. Fell to the floor. He was holding me down. We were both yelling. His swinging, lashing, leather strap wrapped around my face like a bullwhip.

My mother had been outside, but now I heard her running across the porch. I was crying and pleading for help. She rushed up the stairs, thrust her body between us, and snatched his wrists. He pushed her away and she bounced against the wall, tumbled backwards down the stairs.

A son can't hit a father. Unless a father is hitting a mother.

I lit into him, fists flying, fingers clawing. He backed away in surprise.

Then came the standoff—*heavy breathing, barred fists.* Two angry bulls. On top of the stairs. The same spot on which I had once been waiting, at seven years old, for my brothers to come home and obliterate me.

As I think back now, I can't remember my room the way it was before my brothers' invasion. As if that room, my own true room, was created for the three of us, as if it had never been mine alone.

Any memory of my ownership of this refuge was erased that day of their appearance, that hour. I was an orphan, sneaking in and out at night in the inky icy blackness. I was enmeshed in a paralyzing pool of darkness.

But I had a make-believe walkie-talkie.

The night after squaring off with my father.

I opened my eyes, got out of bed, stood into the room and stared at the blank black walls. After a while, I walked over to where my blue jeans hung on my bedpost and pulled out my make-believe walkie-talkie. I took it in my hand and went over to the window, pulled up the Venetian blind and, in the light from the street lamps, searched the foil for the invisible switch. I flipped down my thumb and clicked on my tongue. "Gutkind to Lindenbaum. Gutkind to Lindenbaum. Are you there, Marc Lindenbaum, are you there?"

At first, there was nothing, except for the buzzing of our secret frequency, and then suddenly I felt the walkie-talkie warming in my hands. "This is Lee Gutkind calling Marc Lindenbaum. This is Lee Gutkind calling Marc Lindenbaum. Are you there, Marc Lindenbaum? Over."

Then came a crackling, as if somebody were rolling up paper, followed by wheezing and coughing and more rolling up and crackling of paper, and then came Lindenbaum. "Yes I am here, Lee Gutkind, but you know I won't be here for too much longer."

"This is why I am calling to talk with you, Lindenbaum. I want you to take me with you. Over."

"I am afraid I can't do that, Gutkind. Over."

"Why not, Lindenbaum, why not? Over."

"Because death is not a voluntary thing. When you die at my age you have to be selected. We are the chosen few. Over."

"Oh yeah? And who the hell does that? The selection, I mean. Who chooses the few? Over."

"Who do you think, Gutkind? Who do you think has the power to decide who lives and who dies? Over."

I knew whom Marc Lindenbaum was talking about because I had encountered God a number of times in the recent past. I hadn't realized right away that this figure I began sighting was God, Himself, or even God-like, but I began to notice that a helicopter seemed to shadow Marc Lindenbaum everywhere he went. An old man with a long-flowing white beard and bright red nose piloted the helicopter. He looked like Jesus Christ, Santa Claus, Uncle Sam, and Woody Allen—combined. But after a while it became crystal clear to me that the helicopter shadowing Lindenbaum, hovering above his head, could be piloted by nobody else but the Big Man—the supreme hotshot—God Himself, the ultimate sponsor of everyone on earth, the man who made our unhappiness possible.

I could always hear God in His helicopter before I saw Him; it was beating from a long way off, sharp and dull at the same time, *clopp-clopp-clopp*, thudding like a lumberjack's chopping axe. The sound came on quickly, growing louder and faster, creating a terrible, vibrating racket. Then suddenly it came into view, bursting out of the clouds, swooping down into the neighborhood and situating itself directly over Marc Lindenbaum's head. The helicopter in which God sat was the biggest, loudest machine I had ever seen or heard. I could see or hear nothing else in the whole wide world now but God and His helicopter, swooping down on Marc Lindenbaum. Yet, whenever it appeared, Lindenbaum would not hear it or see it. He would just stand there, hands on his hips, staring at me, wondering what I was listening to or seeing. I was astounded.

I once caught a glimpse of God sitting inside His helicopter in a red velvet cockpit throne dressed in a white robe with a white beard and white buck shoes, the kind that tennis players or golfers like to wear when they get all dressed up. I knew who He was right away. A person so magnificent could be no one else, but God. I took out my make-believe walkie-talkie, clicked on the invisible switch and radioed up to Him. "Gutkind to God, Gutkind to God, Gutkind to God."

He didn't answer, neither signal nor word. But I knew for a fact that God had received my transmission because I saw him shrugging his shoulders, shaking His head sadly back and forth, as if to say, "I'm sorry. But I am simply not ready to talk with you at this particular time. Try again later."

I have tried often over the years to contact him, hoping he might one day be ready to respond to my questions, but I haven't had much luck.

Marc Lindenbaum died not long after Kiner and I befriended him, as everyone knew he would, and my vision of God's helicopter, the all-knowing sage, died with him, until that day, perhaps thirty-five years later, when Daniel was allegedly abused near my house.

God was a constant topic of conversation with Daniel. "I don't believe in God because I can't see Him. Who made the television or the telephone or trees? Who made the roads? People say that's God. Where is God? Why can't I see who He is? If God really does exist, then that man in black would not have molested me," Daniel told me that afternoon, as we sat in my car in the alley viewing the scene of the alleged crime.

I pointed upward at the hospital helicopter hovering above us. "When I was a kid your age, I used to think that God was a helicopter pilot," I told him. "He clopped around through my neighborhood, hovering over people and deciding whether they would live or die or whether they would be popular or smart in school. I tried to talk to Him, but he always ignored me."

Daniel looked at me quizzically. "You thought God was a helicopter pilot?"

I nodded. "I actually thought God was both the helicopter and the pilot rolled into one. It was a spiffy helicopter and it had all kinds of gadgets, including death bomb missiles, which He shot at people He wanted to kill."

"If the missiles detonated, you were dead?" Daniel asked.

"If the missiles were on target, you were selected to die. God programmed each of the death bomb missiles so that people would die when the people who loved them least expected or wanted them to die."

"You're saying God was mean?"

"I'm saying that God was a motherfucker when He wanted to be," I replied.

"God is the father," Daniel said. "That's what the minister at church says that the Bible says. God is the father of everybody, including Jesus Christ."

"Do you think that God is the father of the man in black who molested you?" I asked Daniel.

"How could He be?" Daniel asked.

"How could He not?"

Daniel laughed for the first time since we had come together on the steps of the house. "And people say that *I am crazy*," he said. "I think you could use some Prozac yourself."

"There's no doubt about that," I told him. "Now you see the truth. Everyone of us is nearly over the edge."

After a while, I backed down the alley and once again headed for the convenience store. A police van was sitting in the parking lot, engines idling. Out of the corner of my eye, I could see two officers, both women, eating a take-out lunch and listening to their radio. Daniel did not see the police van, but its presence provided me with a direction, right or wrong. "Well, Dan, this is your chance," I said, pointing at the white van with its large blue and gold official seal. "We could approach these officers and tell them what happened."

Daniel did not hesitate. "Yes," he said with conviction. We got out of the car, walked across the parking lot, and knocked on the window of the van. "I was molested by a man dressed in black," Daniel said.

Almost instantly, the officer on the driver's side activated her walkie-talkie. Announcing the specific location, I heard her summarize Daniel's story to her sergeant, using the word that both Daniel and I had studiously avoided: "A reported rape."

Within five minutes, the entire parking lot was ringed with police vehicles. Daniel was asked to tell his story twice more, once by a sergeant and then by a medic, and with each telling Daniel became more distraught. He buried his face in my chest and began sobbing uncontrollably, especially when the medic attempted to take him in the ambulance to the hospital for the long and intense physical examination required.

Not surprisingly, investigating police discovered no evidence on the reported scene, behind the bushes in the alley. Nor did the doctors discover any sign of sexual violation or activity on Daniel. But to this day, Daniel sticks by his story. He doesn't care whether anyone believes him or not. He alone is well aware of the truth of this and many other similar incidents of molestation and abuse he has reported. The abuse of his early years has been frequently confirmed, though. His parents isolated Daniel alone in a rented rooming house where neighbors, cousins, and even elder siblings, violated him regularly. The rooming house burned down. Daniel suffered serious neurological damage when the ceiling collapsed on his head.

The system that rescued him wasn't any too kind to Daniel, either. During his adolescence, Daniel was transferred from facility to facility twenty-one times; his counselors and support workers, his only parental figures besides me, changed every six months and sometimes less. Even the psychiatrist, who had rescued him from a near-vegetative state in a county mental hospital, had been fired from the facility and abruptly taken off his case the evening before Daniel had attempted to kill himself. So if Daniel conjures up a few unlikely stories, I can't blame him too much, and I honestly don't mind having a relationship with someone whose perceptions I don't always accept, literally.

I identify with Daniel. The sharp differences in our backgrounds significantly limit my ability to understand the daily realities of his life, but I am starkly aware of the thin line that separates the fortunate and unfortunate of this world.

For a long time, I never knew if, when my father reached out toward me, he was going to punch or caress me. The child I continue to have nightmares about—that little boy stranded in the basement darkness and beaten with a strap by an enraged father—was me. Too often we exaggerate the differences between the mentally ill and others who are judged to be sane, but not very nice. The blurred gray lines between criminality and acceptability have never been defined.

This was the thesis of my book *Stuck in Time: The Tragedy of Childhood Mental Illness*, which told the story of helpless children enmeshed in the mental health system. For part of my research, I immersed myself, off and on for nearly three years, in an adolescent bipolar ward of a psychiatric hospital while, on the outside, I documented Daniel's discouraging life. The title comes from a scene in Kurt Vonnegut's novel, *Slaughterhouse Five*.

The protagonist, Billy Pilgrim, entered his living room, turned on the television, and suddenly became "slightly unstuck in time," an event that enabled him to watch the late movie on TV—an epic about American bomber pilots in World War II—backward. This was a marvelously therapeutic experience: American planes, riddled with bullet holes and bloodied men, took off from an English airfield backward and flew backward to France, where they were confronted by German fighters, which soaked bullets back into gun barrels protruding from their cockpits.

The Americans followed the fighters to Germany, backward, where fire and debris were siphoned up from the earth into big bombs. As the backward procession continued, the bombs were stacked on racks in England, then transported on ships to the United States where American pilots were transformed into high school kids. The movie subsequently reversed direction, but Billy Pilgrim speculated that if the backward momentum had continued, Adolph Hitler might have been a baby and Adam and Eve reborn.

This is what I wished for Daniel, for Marc Lindenbaum—and what, for many years, I always wished for myself; that somehow, with the flick of a make-believe walkie-talkie switch or the wave of a Ralph Kiner baseball-bat magic wand, we too might become unstuck in time, triggering a journey backward to a much more hopeful starting point.

Starting over never happened for Marc, who died too soon for magic or medical science to intervene. And life has not yet come together for Daniel, either, who, at twenty-five and now on his own, continues to hop from place to place, seeking a home and a familylike support system. As for me, today, who and what I was before this or any other previous moment will forever be shaded and shaped by the events that led to this intersection between past and present.

Forever Fat

When I was growing up, food was my first support system. When adults asked about my hobbies, I always spread my arms to show my expansive huskiness before replying: "Eating." My parents called me "the human garbage can." Anything they put on my plate, I would devour. Anything left on other plates I would also devour. Eating when I felt tension, excitement, fear—virtually any emotion—was the therapy and comfort I turned to.

For my bar mitzvah at age thirteen, I was fitted in a forty-four "husky" suit at Kaufmann's Department Store in downtown Pittsburgh. "Husky" was Kaufmann's polite term for overweight kids. My mother chose brown wool tweed for me—for durability. But it was very scratchy—bulky—which made me feel and look even more ungainly and constricted than I was.

My bar mitzvah was my first—and last time—up on the stage with the bigwigs of the synagogue. The cantor was short and stocky, with a bushy gray mustache, heavily fortified by springy, serpentine nose hair. When I first met him at Hebrew school, when I started preparing for bar mitzvah, he reached under my jacket and poked the fat around my ribs, as if he were checking to see if I was inflated. "What's your favorite food?" he asked, surveying my lumpy body.

I wasn't sure how to answer, since foods alone didn't give me pleasure and comfort; it was the process of eating I craved. But I picked a type of food I knew would appeal to a Jewish clergyman. "Chopped liver," I said.

Which is how he had greeted me the morning of my bar mitzvah.

I was called by my Hebrew name to the podium. I left my seat in the front row of the congregation, where my parents were sitting, and walked up the steps. The half-dozen synagogue elders assisting with the services moved aside, allowing me to squeeze into the inner circle with the cantor and the rabbi. We huddled around the holy Torah—a precious scroll with hand-inscribed lettering on which were recorded the ancient words of the Talmud.

It was normally hot in the synagogue—the old people who came for Sabbath services preferred the heat—but up on the stage, under the lights, it was at least twenty degrees warmer. I was sweating in my brown wool suit by the time the three of us wrestled the velvet cover from the Torah and rolled it out on the table in front of us. And I was squirming; annoying little woolly itch-pincers were erupting all over my body.

As I stood staring at the Torah, the cantor leaned into me, his arm around my shoulder, and pinched my cheek between his thumb and forefinger. His mustache tickled my neck as he leaned into our inner circle and whispered loudly to the rabbi and the elders behind us, "Chopped liver."

I can't imagine that anyone in that tight little group knew exactly what the cantor was referring to. The elders stared at me, smiling tentatively; traditionally in Jewish culture, any sentence in which the phrase "chopped liver" appears, when it is not specifically re-lated to food, is usually funny and denigrating. Borscht Belt come-dians would ask audiences, "What am I, chopped liver?" meaning, "Why are you staring at me as if I am some sort of holiday platter; why aren't you laughing at my jokes?" At which point the audience would respond with hilarity, even though they could have recited this comeback and every variation by heart.

But the rabbi, Dr. Bernard Poupko, a distinguished scholar of Jew-ish studies with a massive hooked nose and a pointed goatee, was only temporarily amused. A smile flashed across his face, but then his mood shifted—I didn't know why—and his friendly manner disappeared.

Immediately, he reached out and dug his fingers into my shoul-ders—and squeezed. At first I thought that he too was feeling to see if my bulkiness was authentic. But the rabbi began to squeeze harder. He wouldn't let go. I tried to maneuver my shoulder for relief, but his grip was like steel.

I couldn't understand what was happening. Was this some ancient Hebraic ritual I had missed in my studies—paralyzing the bar mitzvah boy prior to his induction into adulthood? The rabbi's small black eyes pierced into me, as he squeezed. The pain was intense. I began leaning over; my knees were buckling. Eventually it dawned on me that he was trying to tell me something. I followed the downward direction of his eyes until I recognized the problem. Droplets of sweat were falling from my forehead and cheeks and landing on the sacred parchment of the Torah.

What was I to do? I was confused, about to panic. Was I, suddenly now a man, expected to make a holy connection with God who would somehow make my perspiration, before tainting the parchment of the Torah, disappear? Could I concentrate enough to will myself to stop sweating in my brown wool hothouse of a suit? I couldn't move my arms to wipe my brow without literally pushing the rabbi away. Clearly, he was not inclined to release me. And I couldn't step backward because the cantor was behind me and the synagogue elders were behind him; this was a very cramped space.

But the worst part was that I came to realize that it was I who was taking up most of the room at the podium. It dawned on me that I was considerably bigger than any of the men with whom I was sharing center stage, although every one of them were at least five times my age.

All of a sudden, I felt humiliated and, worst of all, ridiculous. The word *buffoon* popped into my head at that moment. It had been a vocabulary word we had studied the previous year, in sixth grade, and a word used on television to describe the exploits of the professional wrestlers of the era, as in "Haystack Calhoun, the six-hundred-pound buffoon." Up to that point, I had been aware that I was a heavy child. But my mother had always assured me that I was "big-boned"—not fat. I had never considered myself unsightly—until that moment.

Throughout this time, the rabbi had not uttered a word. Perhaps he was waiting to see what I would do—or say. But after a while, a nostril curled up in disdain, as he reached into his back pocket with his free hand, took out his handkerchief, and calmly blotted the ancient hand-scribed letters on the parchment that I had contaminated. He wiped his brow and blew his nose with a honk that echoed throughout the synagogue, then released my shoulder and stepped back from the Torah, thus disconnected from me, as if he was washing his hands of my touch and obliterating my presence, then and forever, from his memory.

Relieved, but shaken and embarrassed, I stumbled and squeaked my way through the small section of the Torah I was supposed to read—a two-minute exercise I had practiced for the past six months. I had no idea what the words meant, and I had long ago given up asking my teachers to translate what I was saying. "On your bar mitzvah day you are talking to God," the cantor once told me. "He will know what you are telling him. It is nothing for you to worry about."

But if God had understood what I was really praying at that moment, in my heart, behind the words of the Torah, and had been inclined to grant me my bar mitzvah boy wishes, I would have immediately and forever disappeared. I did not want to be a part of the world anymore; nothing could have pleased me more than to have been dead.

Considering what had happened and how terrible and embarrassed I felt, I might have resolved to lose weight. But at the reception after the bar mitzvah, I rushed over to the bagels, the smoked salmon, the herring in sour-cream sauce and, of course, the chopped liver. I should have turned and walked away from all of those delicious deli treats. I did not, after all, want to look or feel like a buffoon. But when I saw the food, sprawling over the tables on heaping platters, beckoning to me, I couldn't resist.

I continued to feel the expression of outrage in the rabbi's piercing fingers on my shoulders, as well as my own unceasing humiliation for many months thereafter, but that afternoon, through eating—and eating—my anxiety slowly subsided.

In tenth and eleventh grade I had my first girlfriend, Jane Golomb, who was nearly as chunky as me. My classmates made up a jingle, based on Tennessee Ernie Ford's hit song:

Sixteen tons and what-do-you-got?
Jane and Lee lying on a cot.

I weighed 220 pounds the year I graduated high school. I was five feet, nine inches—my full height. In the car on the way to our high school prom, my date, Patsy Guttman—Jane ran away with one of my classmates, Irving Wnuk, to Kingston, New York, to have a baby and is now a successful practitioner of electrolysis in Squirrel Hill, the neighborhood where we grew up—confessed she had accepted my invitation because she was madly in love with my friend Steven Mayerstein, with whom we were double-dating. I was a "nice boy," but too fat to take seriously.

I spent the entire night watching Patsy chase Mayerstein. Late in the evening, I found them in the men's room, necking, a wing of Patsy's floor-length evening dress dipped into a urinal.

My only other best friend in high school, Mel Herwald, I met on the first day of chemistry class my junior year. He was new to the school. Herwald immediately befriended me by changing his name to "Hebwald," thereby displacing Jerome Heffner in the alphabetic order of seating. "Why did you do that?" I asked.

"To sit next to you," he replied.

I couldn't understand why Herwald sought out my company. I had absolutely no redeeming qualities. I was not only fat but also unfashionable. Everyone who was anyone in my class wore India madras plaid shirts and khaki pants with buckles on the back—the "Ivy" look—while I came to school every day in white T-shirts and dungarees that, my mother said, were the only trousers available in husky sizes. My grades were below average, I lived on the wrong side of the tracks, and I was frequently sullen. So when Herwald chose me as a friend, seemingly arbitrarily and spontaneously, I was forever grateful—and obedient.

One night Herwald took me for a ride in his father's v-8 Chrysler with push-button automatic transmission. We smoked cigarettes and talked about the girls in our classes. Suddenly he gunned his engine and drove directly up onto the front lawn of a small brick house on a quiet street we had been cruising. We parked on the patio. "Get out and knock on the door," he said.

"Who lives here?"

"It's a surprise."

"This doesn't seem right."

"I thought we were friends," he said, a sure way to entice me into doing his bidding. "C'mon, don't be chicken," he added. "Knock on the door."

I felt compelled to do what he asked. I was afraid he would not want to be my friend if I didn't listen to him. When I got out of the car I noticed that Herwald's father's Chrysler had torn a muddy slick through the lawn and smashed the manicured shrubs that encircled the yard. Feeling exposed and victimized, I was about to jump back in the car and demand a quick getaway, when the front door opened. It was Miss Hanlon, our chemistry teacher. When Mel pulled away, leaving me on the porch, laughing hysterically, I knew I was in trouble.

But I couldn't resist Herwald's interest in me. Later that year, he asked me to deliver a "surprise" birthday present to his girlfriend's dad, a gift-wrapped box of horse manure collected at the local riding stable. The man thanked me when I handed him the box with a cheerful "Delivery for you!" and gave me a dollar tip.

I might have gotten away unidentified, but unfortunately, I was the only kid in high school who wore red Hush Puppies. My father, a "shoe dog," a person who has devoted his life to the shoe business, had assured me that red Hush Puppies would soon be at the cutting edge of fashion. Everyone would be wearing red Hush Puppies and I would be way out ahead of the pack. Little did he know that it would take forty years for a Hush Puppies renaissance to occur in the United States—and never in Pittsburgh. When Mel's girlfriend's dad reported me to the principal, as did Miss Hanlon after our evening visit to her house, they both referred to me as the fat kid with red feet whom everyone called "Slim."

I hated being called Slim. But it was ten times more acceptable than

"Joogie." When I was a baby, my grandmother Ida—my mother's mother—rocked me gently up and down in her lap, chanting repeatedly, "Ah jooga-jooga, ah jooga-jooga," to put me to sleep. It was a song with no meaning. But pretty soon everyone at home was calling me Joogie.

"Lee," a girl's name derived from my grandmother, Leah, my father's mother, who died when my father was a teenager, was the name they used when they were angry. I hated "Lee" as much as I hated "Slim" and "Joogie."

Playing off the pronunciation of my last name (Good-kind), the advisor of the boys club I belonged to in high school, a man called Iggy, a Yiddish reference to his oversized ears, nicknamed me "The Gook"—long before its later reference to the Vietcong. Iggy, who owned Kahn-Morris Beverage Company, which distributed beer and soft drinks to stores and private customers, introduced me to Harry Coke, Paul Pepsi, and Buddy the Squirt Man, truck drivers for the bottling companies licensed in the area to manufacture the beverages they delivered to Iggy to sell. I didn't like being called "The Gook"; it was an ugly word with a distasteful sound. Like "goop"—which was a direct reflection of my fatness—flabby and unsightly, a buffoon, sticky and disgusting. But I loved being with Iggy and his friends and to my great relief and surprise, none of those men ever made reference to my weight or my voracious appetite.

I always tried to arrive at Iggy's for lunch, even if sometimes this would be my second or third lunch of the day. Bundles of orange-brown butcher paper were spread over Iggy's desk which, when opened, exploded in pungent aromas of corned beef, pastrami, pickled tongue, pickles the width of your fist. Conversations focused on women, how to get them, what to do when you succeeded, how to save face when rejected. Other subjects included adventures from World War II and the Korean conflict, and sad stuff about divorce, debt, and death—the "3D's." Frequently, Ray Riddle, the Canada Dry driver, brought in stag films and showed them on Iggy's ancient projector in the Kahn-Morris basement. It was unfortunate that such activities were programmed around lunch—I didn't really need to eat—but the sensory gratification, the taste and smell—enhanced the excitement of the sexual adventures on film. Sharing baskets of French fries smothered in ketchup and chicken salad sandwiches squishing with mayonnaise while watching oral sex was titillating and hilarious; we all screamed and moaned with nervous pleasure.

Iggy said that if I were going to eat, drink, and watch stag films like the big guys, then I would have to be the official bottle sorter at Kahn-Morris. Empty bottles were worth money for recycling. A case of Canada Dry quarts—twelve bottles in a big, heavy, wooden box— was worth sixty cents credit for Iggy. A case of seven- or twelve-ounce Coke bottles netted forty-eight cents. Customers came into the distributorship with a variety of bottles dumped in cases, cardboard boxes, paper bags, and bushel baskets. Piles of bottles were waiting on back porches of Kahn-Morris customers for Ronnie and Clayton, Iggy's drivers, to pick up. Kids brought in bottles one or two at a time, for pennies and nickels. These were dumped on the floor in the middle of the truck bay.

Beer or soda left at the bottom of the bottles spilled on my hands, pant legs, and shoes. The longer the bottles sat in the truck bay or on customers' back porches, in dank basements, or back alleys, gutters, and garbage cans, the stickier and the more aromatic they got. Flies and hornets, spiders, beetles, and worms concealed themselves inside. I was continuously subject to sneak attacks.

Once a wasp crawled into the Coke bottle from which I was drinking, and I accidentally swallowed it. I looked for it in the toilet every night thereafter for weeks on end, holding my nose and poking my floating feces with a pencil, examining it with great intensity. Eventually I concluded that the wasp wasn't dead; it was feeding inside of me and becoming more abrasive as it ravaged my stomach wall. I could feel its stinger stabbing my insides in repeated angry assaults, like the rabbi's steely fingers, or so I thought, until the doctor told my mother that the pain I was experiencing was unrelated to the swallowed wasp, long ago excreted. I was suffering from a peptic ulcer, a product of emotional stress, an unusual diagnosis for an adolescent. Standard treatment at the time included at least a quart of warm milk a day, plus supplemental milkshakes, custards, and puddings. So I got fatter, while, between meals and snacks, my anxiety increased.

Ronnie was Clayton's nephew. They were both black.

I had never associated with black men before. In my grandparents' and parents' world, black people were (in Yiddish) "schvartzes" who cleaned your house or did other dirty work. At my father's shoe store, the colored men would come once a week to carry the trash out of the basement and haul it in their truck to the dump. Directed by my father, I stationed myself in the basement, pretending to be taking inventory or sweeping the floor, while I guarded the merchandise on the shelves so that the trash men could not steal anything.

I hated doing this; it was so insulting to the trash men, and there was no evidence that they had any intention of stealing. They seemed nice, rather exotic to a sheltered person like me, singing and joking in a run-on word-scrambled language I could not fully comprehend, breaking out in blasts of laughter that I couldn't help but realize were directed toward me. At the end, their job done, the trash gone, the floor swept clean, their garbled language suddenly and miraculously jelled, ringing with unsettling clarity, as they slammed the door behind them and shouted, "Goodbye watcherboy. See you next week."

I left Pittsburgh on the Greyhound bus to Atlantic City, New Jersey, a few weeks after high school graduation. From there we would be taken to the United States Coast Guard Training Station at the very tip of Cape May where I would join company Alpha-48. My ID number was 2007–435. My dog tags, my first medal of maturity, jingled and bounced from my neck.

Enlistment not only allowed me to escape from Pittsburgh, but also put to an end all my humiliating high school names. In the military, one becomes anonymous. You are called "private," "cadet," "soldier," "sailor," "seaman." The objective is to fit in—not to be singled out. The Coast Guard had not been my first, second, third, or fourth choice of enlistment; it was the only service to accept me at my weight. The recruiting officers for the marines and the air force had laughed when I told them I wanted to enlist and they looked at me up and down like I was some sort of animal in a zoo.

In the military, I discovered that others, aside from Jews, blacks, and fat people, were resented and hated. My first day in boot camp, I was accosted by one of the largest men I had ever seen, Bob Ezell from Gainesville, Florida, who was lean and muscular and nearly seven feet tall. Ezell grabbed me by the collar and lifted me onto my toes. "I'm a Southern Baptist," he said to me. "What the fuck is your religion?"

"Jewish," I told him. My voice was squeaky. I braced myself and waited for the onslaught of kicks and punches as punishment for the money-lending, Christ-killing sins of my ancestors. But Ezell lowered me slowly and carefully into my bunk and then straightened the collar of my shirt, with a smile and a sigh. "As long as you're not Catholic," he said.

There was one black person in the company, Willard Mixon. Chief Petty Officer O'Reilly, our company commander, used Mixon as an example of how sailors were supposed to exercise self-control, no matter what sort of temptation or provocation occurred. Frequently, during inspection, right before our regular marching drill, O'Reilly, a short, stout Irishman, stuck his face into Mixon's chin, peered up into his eyes and yelled, "You fucking nigger. C'mon, beat my ass. You hate my guts, don't you, you, nigger? You black motherfucker."

O'Reilly went on and on, repeating his taunting war dance a half-dozen times a week, but Mixon never flinched. He stared through Chief Petty Officer O'Reilly's flushed forehead as if the man didn't exist. Mixon had long ago programmed himself to deaden his senses when people were hurtful or abusive. He could not pretend that O'Reilly wasn't abusing him in the most despicable way imaginable, but I admired how Mixon refused to show any anger, weakness, or emotion. He was a rock. I briefly considered trying to befriend Mixon; we might have something in common.

But I realized that my own problems paled in the face of the ferocious hatred and disdain Mixon was forced to confront. I was also white and privileged—he would see me that way. Being a fatty, a Jew, and a misfit was hardly comparable to being a nigger motherfucker.

I had read James Baldwin's *Notes of a Native Son* not long before enlisting. I had been a voracious reader throughout high school; my only refuge from the mean-spiritedness of the kids in school was the library. I discovered Baldwin because of news articles concerning his exit from America to Paris—an idea that inspired my enlistment in the Guard. It wasn't Paris, but leaving Pittsburgh that obsessed me—never coming back until I was no longer Lee Gutkind, that fat fucker quintessential victim who sucked up alienation like a sponge.

Baldwin was my age, maybe nineteen or twenty, when he too had run from his family and the shroud of unhappiness that enveloped his life. One day at The American Diner in Trenton, New Jersey, he was denied service—"We don't serve Negroes here"—and it drove him into a rage. With the repetition of that phrase ringing in his head "like a thousand bells of a nightmare," he marched down the block to the fanciest restaurant in town, a place "where not even the intercession of the Virgin would cause me to be served," and staged an anger-crazed sit-in. Eventually, after hurling a pitcher of water at a frightened waitress, who had also recited the "We don't serve Negroes here" mantra, Baldwin regained a measure of emotional equilibrium and fled. I realized that the raging, pent-up hatred Baldwin (and Mixon?) harbored was impenetrable to an outsider—a white person, like me—and it would not have surprised me if Mixon, a time bomb like Baldwin, would have suddenly one day lost control and beaten O'Reilly to the pulp he deserved to be.

But as time passed, O'Reilly's onslaughts began to fade and Mixon miraculously became one of O'Reilly's personal aides, frequently being released from duty in order to do favors for him, like spit-shine his shoes or dash to the PX on errands for cigarettes or soda. Eventually Mixon was appointed to the base drill team, a small, specially trained cadre of highly disciplined sailors who lived and trained in a separate part of the compound. He was no longer under O'Reilly's supervision. Mixon was a natural choice for the drill team—he marched with dignity and impeccable precision. But the fact that he might have never been given the opportunity had he lowered himself to O'Reilly's level by responding to his insults and taunts, struck home.

I had no idea how much emotional energy Mixon's self-control had cost him; he too might have had a bleeding ulcer just by containing all of his anger and hatred inside. But his quiet and subtle victory over Chief Petty Officer O'Reilly was a model to remember. Mixon was regularly taunted and abused, but he never lost his dignity—a part of him that eventually earned the admiration of the entire company and won freedom from O'Reilly. Soon Mixon would leave boot camp—a full-fledged seaman—and, if he chose to, he could seek revenge on O'Reilly. I doubted if he did. He would not have given O'Reilly the satisfaction of letting him know that his taunting had been fruitful or that his bigotry could have in any way been interpreted as justified.

Watching Mixon, I realized that I was missing the key ingredient—the self-respect that made the words and taunts directed at me in my own life irrelevant. Not that Mixon didn't care or wasn't affected by the way in which Chief Petty Officer O'Reilly treated him, but he recognized O'Reilly for the bigot he was and knew how shallow and limited his prejudices made him. He outfoxed O'Reilly by believing in himself. While I lacked solutions to my own personal insecurities, I realized that my search for respect must begin inside of me with self-awareness developing into self-assurance. People might someday respect me, but not before I learned respect for myself.

I had assumed, as did most of my friends and family, that in the U.S. Coast Guard I would have an easy time of it, physically. After all, they were the shallow-water sailors. Little did I know that because we were operating on the coast (guarding our shores from enemy aggression), we were always running like hell on land instead of floating in a boat like true seamen.

A favorite drill in basic training was triggered by a signal on the bell tower—three staccato chimes. At that moment, we recruits, wherever we were standing, whatever we were doing, were obliged to grab our pieces (M-I rifles) and bayonets and dash to meet an invading enemy and do combat in the water. Traditional Coast Guard boot camp was twelve weeks versus the army's nine-week stint. This was because people who came into "the Guard" were usually in inferior physical condition, and also because we had more instructional classes, such as semaphore, maritime law, and so on.

After twelve weeks of basic, I was the only member of my company to not graduate and join a unit. I had lost a good deal of weight at this point—and was certainly as fit as I had ever been—having been forced to march around the compound endlessly, do thousands of push-ups and sit-ups and run and dive maniacally through the U.S. Marine-style obstacle course. Six meals a day were not an option. Breakfast, lunch, and dinner were mandated, whether you wanted to eat or not; snacks were disallowed. Needless to say, the food was not as appealing as my mother's cooking or Iggy's lunches. In "The Guard," I learned to work harder and eat less.

But no matter how hard or how often I tried, I could not seem to pass the rope test. This was a rope, fifty feet high, with knots spaced evenly for handholds; I had to climb to the top and then control my descent. There were other ways of boarding an invading ship, but when a rope is the only answer, a Coast Guardsman must be able to do it. Every night after supper, I was tested, and every night I failed.

After boot-camp graduation ceremonies, I said goodbye to my fellow recruits, assigned to units across the country and abroad. I, however, would be anchored to the boot-camp base until I passed the rope test. "We will keep you in this compound," Chief Petty Officer O'Reilly assured me, "for however long it takes."

During the day I worked with a maintenance crew—men who were incarcerated in the brig for minor offenses—inside a large abandoned furnace, chiseling away at the burnt-in soot and debris, without seeing natural light between breakfast and lunch and lunch and supper. At that time, masks were unheard of. I breathed in the coal dust in the morning and coughed it out at night. Working so long and hard while breathing all of that sooty material, by day's end I lacked the energy and determination to climb the rope or even to work out with free weights to strengthen my upper body. I began to think I would serve my entire hitch as a "boot." The rope test was beyond me.

This went on for weeks. At night, instead of working out, I went to the base recreation center, which essentially was a large pool hall with a bar (beer only) and a bunch of televisions. Despite not liking pool—I have never been able to play too well—I thoughtlessly devoted my evening hours to watching others play, sipping Pepsi Cola, and wondering what the hell was going to become of me. Memories of home where I was "Slim," "Joogie," and "The Gook" were suddenly more palatable than before; Pittsburgh might be better than being cooped up in a military base chiseling soot out of the bowels of furnaces with a bunch of ne'er-do-wells. But even this was a moot point. I was trapped here by the rope test.

In the recreation hall one Saturday afternoon, after some weeks of idleness, I wandered aimlessly toward a door in the back of the room near the head. A plaque, like it was some long-forgotten monument, said "Library."

The door was locked. After a couple of inquiries, I discovered that anyone wanting to use the library had to sign out a key at the pool-hall desk. It had been so long since anyone had requested the key that it had been misplaced; the Shore Patrol had to unlock the door for me. Later, since I was the only person using the library, the Shore Patrol, sick and tired of being interrupted every night, gave me my own key. The books I found in the library were of no great surprise—the same stuff I had been reading at home: Hemingway's Nick Adams stories, Frank Slaughter, who wrote dozens of novels about physicians in every conceivable milieu, Arthur Miller's *Death of a Salesman* (I identified with Biff, not an admirable character, but a stupendous nickname), *Marjorie Morningstar*, *The Diary of Anne Frank*, *Huckleberry Finn*. James Baldwin was noticeably absent.

But here, in this alien atmosphere, I found these stacks of dusty books to be of great solace because they reminded me of where I had been in my life in Pittsburgh, my dissatisfaction, and what I was doing in the military—trying to escape my past and find a new direction. More than that, books had been a refuge—my private way of forgetting that I was the fattie called "Slim" with the ostentatious red shoes, suckered into doing Melvin Herwald's dirty work. I had been unable to read since enlisting in the military. Silence and privacy were virtually impossible while sharing space with ninety stinking, farting, snoring, pissing, Homo sapiens. Your every movement—whatever you did—invited a host of daily witnesses.

Thus it was significant that books, this library, allowed a level of privacy, a place to close the door, sit in a soft chair and think, with no one talking or telling you what to do or forcing you to salute. Books were stories, and the stories I read took me to another dimension of time and place where people, some of whom I could identify with, were confronting problems similar to those plaguing me.

My involvement in the stories of other peoples' lives, real or make-believe, helped me assess and eventually reshape my own priorities. Here was Phillip Roth's protagonist in *Goodbye Columbus* frustrated by his inability to be accepted in a world, ironically, he knew in his heart he did not want to be a part of, as I wanted to be accepted in my school and neighborhood, although I did not want to live there. I realized the important and frustrating distinction: that those people weren't any better than I, yet they perceived me as so inferior that they didn't know or wouldn't care that I repudiated them. This was baffling and demoralizing.

Ernest Hemingway's story "Big Two-Hearted River" captured and fortified my search for solitude in the library; I found in the peace and privacy in the library that space Hemingway had savored for healing on the Upper Peninsula. I too was healing (and shrinking) behind those closed doors.

I had no sympathy for Willie Loman, in *Death of a Salesman*, for he was a carbon copy of my father, running from imaginary threats and chasing fantastic dreams. Miller, Roth, and Hemingway could not provide the answers I needed, but the stories they told through the characters they created not only invigorated me but offered a telescopic overview of how people responded when trapped in a warp of isolation and alienation.

Every evening and weekend, in between reading, I found myself beginning to imagine what life would be like when I was out of the military. With the library door locked from the inside, I began doing push-ups and sit-ups—more and more each night. Within weeks, I could feel myself changing. I was getting stronger and more independent. And I was rapidly becoming tired of being called "Seaman"—that wasn't my name. Being anonymous had been a welcome relief, but it no longer satisfied me.

I had no interest in returning to my days of "Slim," "Joogie," or "The Gook." I wasn't any of those people anymore. I was Lee. I could feel myself growing into it for the first time—*Lee—Lee Gutkind—Lee Alan Gutkind—Mr. Lee Alan Gutkind—Dr. Lee Alan Gutkind*—while, physically, I was shrinking. The uniforms I had been given when I enlisted hung from my body like curtains.

What was amazing to me is that I never decided to lose weight; it had just started happening. My clothes were getting looser, and I was getting thinner. It was a transforming experience. As I shed pounds, I also shed anxieties; the discomfort caused by feelings of insecurity—not fitting in—was gradually lifting. And then I began to understand why I was losing weight and feeling better. I wasn't eating as much or as often, and more importantly, I didn't need to. I was working hard, focusing on whatever my commanding officers told me to do, not worrying about what others thought about me. I had rediscovered reading—a solitary activity that provided comfort and an escalating emotional awareness.

I started to get up early in the morning and do additional hundreds of push-ups and sit-ups before reveille. At lunch, instead of eating or smoking, I would take long walks around the compound, reading as I walked. Or I went into the men's room and practiced pull-ups on the toilet stall doors. I stayed behind closed doors because the guys with whom I shared furnace-cleaning duty were in detention because of some criminal act they had committed and not because they were too fat or couldn't pass the rope test. They would not have taken kindly to my "public" display of extra physical training. Their attitude was that we had plenty enough PT in our own routine. In the evening I was back in my private library sanctuary reading and working out.

Under my secret regimen, perhaps no more than six weeks passed before I surprised my superiors and myself by showing up at the gym one evening and literally bounding up the rope from floor to ceiling, almost effortlessly. I touched the top with one sure hand and then skittered down again without using my feet. When I got to the bottom the first time, I showboated by going up again—and back. It was a triumphant moment, not just because I succeeded, but because of the ease with which I pulled it off.

I had worked hard to get to this point—the top of the rope—but when it finally happened, I realized how much I had been missing through the first nineteen years of my life. This was the feeling I was seeking without actually knowing what I was looking for—confidence in myself and in my abilities, a sense of accomplishment in transforming dreams and hopes into objectives and personal victories. I didn't want to be a fat person anymore, a devalued person—an outsider. I wanted to feel and be, inside and out, the new and better me. Up to that point, I had understood the work ethic; that if you applied yourself, you could make great strides and accomplish many goals. But suddenly, the possibilities and potential of my life were much more evident than ever before. Passing the rope test more than satisfied Chief O'Reilly. I could now go on to other postings—and go back home on my first leave—two weeks in Pittsburgh.

The anticipation of returning home was sweet. I could envision the headlines in my parents' favorite local paper, *The Jewish Chronicle:* "Former Fatty Now a New Man." Or, "Lee Gutkind Back in Pittsburgh: Triumphant—and Thin!" I pictured the glory of my return. Wherever I would go, people would see the svelte new me I had become, stand up—and applaud. I weighed eighty pounds less than when I left a year before. It was a miracle that I alone made happen.

I had not told anyone in my letters and weekend phone calls how I had been changing. I know I said I was getting stronger and losing a little weight, but I avoided specific details about how many pounds I had lost or how hard I had worked to make it happen. I wanted the new Lee to be a surprise. When I jumped off the bus at the Greyhound station, I approached my anxious, flustered mother, her eyes darting to the left and right. I stopped a few feet in front of her, spread my arms to embrace her and . . . she walked right by me!

"You don't recognize your own son?" I said.

She turned and looked, as if she had never seen me before, and then began to cry. "Oh my God, what have they done to my child?"

I was delighted by her response.

My family had been shocked when I had been suspended from school after being blamed for ruining Mrs. Hanlon's lawn and shocked again when, the following month, I had delivered the horse manure to Herwald's girlfriend's father. But those acts—and many others during my high school years (I started a fire in the men's room of my Hebrew school the month before my bar mitzvah)—were unproductive and self-destructive. Enlisting in the military and losing nearly eighty pounds were my first acts of what I like to consider my responsible adulthood—an awareness of productive achievement. A dramatic response had been necessary for me to feel that I had made a truly significant impact. And I knew how my mother gossiped. The more she was flabbergasted, the more she would whine and complain to friends and family about her scrawny, emaciated son, thereby spreading the news.

The week I arrived back in town, I got up early the first morning, before sunrise, a practice gained in the military to which I would remain true all my life, and walked the ten blocks to my high school, Taylor Allderdice. The wide concrete stairs from the front door to the sidewalk were daunting; they had always sent a subtle message that somehow told me I didn't belong with the other people learning and socializing beyond the tall, ornate front doors.

My intention was to wait for the teachers to arrive so that I could show them the new me. But I almost immediately realized the folly in this plan. I had gotten a shrieking but reinforcing response from my mother. That was enough. I did not need an ego-stroking experience, and I didn't want to know what other people thought of me. I knew what I thought of myself, which was all that mattered.

After my leave, I was sent to Norfolk, Virginia, for training and then to a few other postings before discharge from active duty. I would serve in the reserves for the next half-dozen years. Not until I returned home for good did I begin to recognize the possibilities of my life. I could go to college and learn more about literature, even though I had barely graduated high school. I finished near the bottom of the lower fifth of my class. And later I realized that I, like Hemingway, Wolfe, and Roth, could write essays, stories—even books, if I tried hard enough and applied myself and retained my patience and a slow but unwavering determination.

The rope test had been a life test. I would never forget—I would never permit myself to forget—that there were few limitations to my potential, as long as I had a goal in mind and I persisted. I could and would climb the rope, any rope, anywhere, no matter how long it might take—how much effort it required.

Along the way, I adopted two ideas—"slogans," if you wish, or "mantras"—that became guiding principles. The first comes from an organ-transplant surgeon I met while doing research for one of my books, *Many Sleepless Nights*, who was talking with a patient waiting—and slowly dying—for an organ for transplant. Paraphrasing Winston Churchill appealing to the British people in 1941 in the darkest days of the German blitzkrieg, the surgeon told his patient: "Never give in, never give up. Never. Never. Never. Ever."

The real quotation, which I later looked up, is a little different, but says essentially the same thing: "Never give in, never give in. Never. Never. Never. Never. In nothing great or small, large or petty, never give in, except to convictions of honor and good sense." But I remember that the patient somehow responded; he managed to live a couple more days—until a heart became available for transplant. I lost touch with him after his surgery, and I don't know if he lived or for how long, but the meaning of the message was clearly imprinted on my mind. I will never give in—and I will never forget how much I might achieve in my life if I continue to try. Not trying means capitulation.

The second image also came from another sick person—an old friend who had battled depression all of his life—and who had attempted to commit suicide by slitting his wrists on the day of his marriage. His new wife discovered him bleeding and nearly dead in the bathroom. Paramedics saved his life. A few weeks later, while visiting him back at home, I asked him why he was able to look so cheerful and how he was managing to project a positive image after all he had been through. He chanted for me the little song he heard in the suicide unit—the ward where every patient was under twenty-four-hour observation—in the psychiatric facility where he had recuperated.

While lying in bed in the dark, the door to his room wide open so that nurses could maintain constant surveillance, he could hear a man singing to himself. This man, he found out later, had lost his wife and child in an auto accident some years ago. He had been driving. Since then he had suffered severe and paralyzing fits of depression. He had frequently tried to hurt himself but, according to the nurses, he always seemed to rally and recover and try to get on with his life. He was strong enough to leave the hospital—frequently—but not strong enough to manage his depression at home for a sustained period of time. His song was simple and relentless, my friend said, and kind of eerie to hear again and again, but the message, so clear and simple, struck home: "Fall down nine times . . . Get up ten."

Years later, when I was going through a period of unhappiness after a divorce and began long-distance running, I put both images together, and developed a silent chant of my own, which I repeated and continued to repeat in times of pressure and stress: "Never give up, never give in, fall down nine times, get up ten."

I realize how silly this sounds, how elementary and predictable, how New Age. And yet, most people I know have baggage to overcome. The most sensible objective is to do anything possible—whatever you can come up with—to think positively about life and not allow events over which you have no control, nor the people behind those events, to drag you down. If a couple of slogans can harness my flailing spirit or remind me of my inherent strength, then why not invoke them?

Processing and confronting baggage from the past is often the more daunting challenge. Just because I am solid and muscular, can lift heavy weights, and run ten miles with no significant effort, doesn't mean that I am not fat. Buried deep down inside is the same old Joogie I was before. I am constantly struggling to remember who I am.

Today, people don't call me Slim or The Gook anymore; now it is Professor, or author, or "The Godfather," thanks to James Wolcott, and, best of all, father or dad. But every morning when I get up and stumble into the bathroom for morning ablutions, the mirror presents a double image. There is me as I am today, a gray but vigorous middle-aged man—a person with purpose and direction and significant accomplishment, considering my rather unimpressive beginnings.

But in that same morning mirror, there is the faded but clearly recognizable image behind me of the blob of a boy in a bulky brown suit, trapped by people who disapproved of me. I wash my hands, I brush my teeth, I floss and shave. I begin my day. But that bar mitzvah boy on the podium in the synagogue stays with me. His fatness is my constant companion—a threat if I do not continue to toe the line, and a ghost anchoring the paranoia of my dungaree days that hound me. Rabbi Poupko's steely fingers are forever digging into my neck.

Anyone who has ever been fat knows that no matter how much weight you lose and how muscular your armor and how long you manage to remain svelte and strong, you will never be thin. You may think you have created an impenetrable façade of slimness; new people in your life may even be shocked when you confide that you are a former flabby fatty. They say, "I can't imagine you as anything else but fit."

But no matter how supportive they may be, lauding you for your transformation, you can't afford to believe them. They cannot see inside you. Inside is where it counts because inside is where your belly will always be bloated. The extent to which you control that fat fucker seeking therapeutic relief through eating inside your body—how you balance the mirror's double image—is a challenge all formerly fat people share.

I have learned that it is fruitless to attempt to obliterate the past. Who you were is who you are. Wherever I go, the fat person, whatever you want to call him, Joogie, Slim, The Gook, can never be forgotten. He is a deep and clinging dimension of my personality, always capable of dragging me down. But I do not fight or deny him. I purposely keep him with me as I go through my day. In this way, I stop him from sneaking up on me when I am least expecting it and making me feel trapped and vulnerable. I refuse to allow myself to forget that boy on the podium, paralyzed in the confusion of adolescence, finding comfort and solace in excessive amounts of food—an escape from reality that could have easily destroyed me.

A History of My Father

About ten years ago, my father decided to write a letter explaining himself. He wrote with a ballpoint pen on lined paper, took it to a local Kinko's for duplication and the post office for mailing. As soon as I opened the envelope, and I realized what my father had done, I tossed it in a drawer. I did not want to read anything my father had to say about how or why he had raised me; I had invested many years in therapy learning to deal with the trauma from his violent outbursts and learning to get on with my life.

But one day, years after I received the letter, and for no particular reason, I dug it out of the file drawer, poured a cup of coffee, and started reading. Surprisingly, it was in no way traumatizing. The fact that my father had frequently whipped me with a leather belt and imprisoned me in the dark behind a locked basement door as punishment for misbehaviors real and imagined never came up. That his temper traumatized the whole family was also never mentioned. He was telling his own side of the story. He wasn't looking at life from anyone else's viewpoint.

My father was born in the Lawrenceville section of Pittsburgh, while two older sisters, Hattie and Ethel, were both born in New York. His father, Isadore, was a real estate agent and a tailor, who also owned a dry goods store. The family lived upstairs. My father's mother, Leah, my namesake, got sick before his tenth birthday, so my father was frequently kept home from school to help operate the store, the only employee. Neither the store nor the quarters above were equipped with electricity. There were gas mantels for light and a pot-bellied stove for heat in the kitchen. Firing up the boiler was permitted only on days they took baths. "I never had toys or a sled," my father writes. "But in the winter I used to slide down the Thirty-fifth Street hill in the snow all the way to the railroad tracks on a garbage can lid." He made a wagon from a buggy he resurrected from a junk pile and a scooter from discarded roller skate wheels.

Leah's diseased liver became more critical over the next few years, but on the day she signed my father's registration for high school, Hebrew Polytechnic, she was sitting up in a wheelchair for the first time in months. When my father returned after school, his mother was dead. It was February 1, 1929, a Friday, and she was buried on a Sunday. As was the custom, most Orthodox Jews did not go to a funeral home, and they did not bury their dead during the Sabbath. So, after sundown on Saturday, Leah's body was transported home from the hospital. "She was laid out in the living room with candles at her head—no coffin," my father wrote. "In the morning, a wooden casket was brought in, covered with a black velvet shawl with a Star of David on it. I can't express my feelings of what that did to me, my mother dead in the living room all night long. Orthodox Jews in heavy black clothing said prayers through the following night. She was buried at Beth David Cemetery, Long Island, New York, on Sunday." From that point on, the family referred to my father as "the orphan."

A few months after his mother's death, my father came home from school. His father was absent, but a cousin directed him to the home of another relative. A wedding had just taken place, and my father arrived in the middle of a celebratory dinner. He was ushered into the room and seated across from a woman he had neither seen nor met before. This was his father's new wife—my father's new mother. Soon after, my father left home and restarted life alone.

He worked in a fruit store, as a Western Union boy delivering telegrams, and sold newspapers and peanuts and football souvenirs, which he designed and made himself, with the appropriate school colors. After graduating high school, he worked in a machine shop and as a draftsman. But this was in the height of the Depression and the company soon went bankrupt. For a while, he sold razor blades, then he began reconditioning used automobile spark plugs, purchased for a penny apiece. My father sanded and repainted them, set the gaps, had special boxes made, which said "Guaranteed Reconditioned," then resold them back to the garages for retail sale to customers. One garage owner, who housed private taxicabs and limousines, offered him a job as a night watchman. My father taught himself to drive by zipping around the garage in the taxis in the middle of the night. Beer trucks owned by the mobster Dutch Schultz were also stored here, making deliveries throughout the city from midnight to five in the morning.

Eventually, he decided to hitchhike to Washington DC to start a new life, but no one would give him a ride. He walked for three hundred miles. Late one night, he knocked on the door of a training camp for boxers in the Blue Ridge Mountains—the only light for miles around—and begged for food. I realized by the date of his letter that this could have been Jack Dempsey's training camp when he was heavyweight champ. I momentarily envisioned my father being taken in by Dempsey's people, fed and cared for and given some sort of janitorial job because he and the champ shared the same first name. Eventually the two Jacks got together and became buddies, which is how my father learned to box, and he was ringside when Dempsey fought his immortal battle with Tunney.

This was my vision—that my father had had an incredible secret life he might reveal that would redeem or explain him in my eyes—but it wasn't true. My father was never ringside at any fight, couldn't fight his way out of a shoe box, and never met anyone famous, except for when Robert Kennedy, on the campaign trail for his brother (another Jack), walked into my father's store to borrow a ladder to get up on a podium. What happened at the training camp was that my father knocked on the door and was turned away. Nearly freezing to death, he huddled in a space between two outbuildings; the following morning, shivering every step, he journeyed to the nation's capital.

Peddling his items in Washington DC wasn't successful or satisfying. In Pittsburgh, you earned respect for working hard and showing evidence of industriousness. There was a certain pride in honest poverty, but in the nation's capital, wealthy people of a variety of cultures looked past the down-and-out as if they did not exist. My father went to New York, lived for a while with his sisters, then met up with two cousins and hitchhiked to Chicago to see the World's Fair. Unfortunately, he can't tell me much of what he did in Chicago at the Fair—or relate any of his adventures on the road. He doesn't even mention the experience in his letter.

After the Chicago World's Fair, my father went to Clarksburg, West Virginia, to work as a clerk in a shoe store. In Pittsburgh for a weekend visit, Jack met Mollie. They were engaged in three months.

One reason for the whirlwind courtship and decision to marry quickly was my father's 150-mile commute from Clarksburg to Pittsburgh, weekends, to be with my mother.

It is difficult to conceive of the passion that propelled him to bump and swerve six hours in his 1928 Ford on Saturday nights, after work, on half-paved West Virginia roads to see my mother on Sundays and then to turn around and retrace his path to be back Monday morning.

I doubt if my parents slept together before marriage, but they obviously experienced a certain amount of intimacy after marriage because my brothers and I were conceived—and we are most definitely and regrettably, by features and temperament, their children.

But in the eighteen years I lived with them, and during all of my visits for family events thereafter, I can't remember Mollie and Jack touching one another. I cannot recall a single handhold, not one kiss.

Perhaps their passions were spent on the teeming Sunday afternoons they shared between my father's mad dashes from Clarksburg to Pittsburgh. Or perhaps I refused to notice their regular physical connection and affection.

I have this tendency to not notice what I don't want to see and forget what I don't want to remember.

But if my parents had become better acquainted before marriage, I am certain I wouldn't be telling this story because, the fact is, I wouldn't exist. My mother and father had little in common.

In the duplex apartment upstairs from my grandparents, where we lived until I was fourteen, you could stand on a ladder in the bedroom closet behind my father's suits and find a window-sized door that opened into a tiny attic. In that space were boxes of heavy black phonograph records, thick with dust: recordings of operas by great performers like Caruso, Lanza, and Ezio Pinza. And there were old long-yellowed books about communism, Zionism, political dissent, filled with his faded pencil scrawl—notes, stars, and exclamation points—evidence of engagement and excitement that were completely unfamiliar in the Jack I knew.

Here was the residue of my father's tragic vulnerability—his compromise with life in order to have the home he was denied by the death of his mother and his father's choice to remarry in such an insensitive and secretive manner.

I understood and accepted the logic and reality of putting his primary passions—opera and Zionism—on the back burner in order to be part of a family and to no longer feel so orphaned. But giving them up entirely meant giving up a piece of his heart—and denying his sons a valuable legacy.

After I read his letter, I asked him why he had walked away from the intellectual pursuits that intrigued him. It was a mistake to ask—I knew right away. Because, instead of providing information to establish a dialogue, he immediately assumed the role of the consummate martyr who did his best as a husband, father, and family provider, but was never properly understood. His litany went on for quite a while, basically blaming my mother's lack of interest, as if he had been browbeaten by her ambivalence into silent intellectual submission.

That my mother was disinterested in opera and politics was true, but I can't imagine she had ever led him to believe anything different. She was neither intellectual nor duplicitous.

In the late 1930s, when Jack and Mollie met (she was twenty years old), women were expected to marry and have children—sooner rather than later. While Jack was obviously not perfect husband material, Mollie has always been a woman who took the easy way out. Not that she was weak; after all, she endured my father for sixty years. But she was neither self-motivating nor self-starting. My mother's decision to stay with my father after I was born was practical, but now I recognized it as the most significant of a long series of personal rejections. My feelings—my literal safety—were being sacrificed because I was less important than someone else, in this case my strongest and most relentless adversary.

Soon after their marriage, my father enlisted in the army to fight the Nazis. He went to boot camp in Birmingham, Alabama, and was shipped overseas. I was born while he was in Europe and was cared for, pampered, by my mother and grandmother, until he returned in 1946. I remember sitting on my mother's lap, rocking in a chair. She was crying when she told me my father was coming home that day. I remember the afternoon he arrived in his wrinkled khakis, his pointed army hat tilted jauntily on the side of his head, a style he maintained with tousle hats, baseball caps, and alpine hats throughout his entire life. While we were all sitting and talking and getting reacquainted, I picked up a yellow porcelain bird on the coffee table. My grandmother had told me repeatedly not to touch this knickknack—it was precious to her. She said it again that afternoon. But I didn't listen. When I fingered it a second and then a third time, my father hit me.

I'll never forget: his first day back from the war, my first interaction with him. I was barely three years old. He slapped my hand once—looked at me sharply, his eyes glowing—and slapped it again. That moment defined the focus of my memories regarding my father. I imagine we had our bonding moments, but my newsreels of life with dad are framed in pain and humiliation beginning with this first scenario, which forever defined our interactions. While I can't deny the inappropriateness of my behavior, my father, a total stranger, was introducing himself and his style of fathering to me. No one had ever touched me before in an ungentle way. I was completely unprepared. I trusted everybody, my mother and grandparents, the neighbors and cousins who came to kiss and tickle me. Then this slap: two pistol shots. The spark of pain on the back of my hand combined with the crisp crack of contact was forever inside me, unrelentingly reminiscent. Each time I found myself in the same room with my father, I braced myself.

After the war, my father worked at the Poll Parrot Shoe Store for Fritz Ehrlich, a very neat, formal German refugee who clicked his heels and bowed when he greeted you. Everyone called him "The Count." My father wasn't crazy about working for Fritz—he wasn't crazy about working *for* anybody—but if you were a shoe dog it was good to be connected to a franchise sponsoring *The Howdy Doody Show* on TV. Howdy wore Poll Parrot shoes, as did Dilly Dally, Buffalo Bob, Princess Summer-Fall-Winter-Spring, Chief Thunderthud, and Mr. Bluster. I, too, wore Poll Parrots with the scuff-proof toe. I also had a pair of brown and white saddle oxfords for dress-up, purchased when my father was working for The Count.

After The Count, my father went to Fink's in Greensburg, Pennsylvania, about thirty-five miles west of Pittsburgh. Greensburg was a prosperous community and Fink's was one of the biggest and most successful shoe stores in the state. Fink's had Buster Brown and Jumping Jacks for kids. They had P.F. Flyers and U.S. Keds canvas shoes. They had Bostonian and Florsheim for men. The black "spade," pointed toes with a shiny, perforated tip, was the most popular style for men and teens, with wing tips a close second. They had Red Cross and Capezio for women. For those awful western Pennsylvania winters, Fink's could supply four-buckle arctic rubber boots, also known as "overshoes," for men, women, and children in three colors.

Fink's had an x-ray machine called a fluoroscope, a big wood-paneled, console-like device, resembling an old-fashioned Victrola. You put on your new shoes and inserted your feet into the left and right openings at the base of the unit. Suddenly you could see the green outline of your feet, as if encased in neon, and judge for yourself how they fit into the new scuff-toe oxfords, if you were a boy, or patent-leather T-straps for girls.

As manager of the store, my father worked six days a week, 10 A.M. to 6 P.M. and until 9 P.M. Wednesday and Saturday nights, while Mr. Fink, who usually appeared during the day only, worked sporadic casual hours. Fink, a tall, severe-looking man with a mustache and a long nose, was fond of my father and wanted to turn over to him part ownership of the store. His children, college-educated professionals, did not want to live in a tiny hick town like Greensburg or labor day and night as shoe dogs. But Mr. Fink would not give my father a share of the business until he made a symbolic but essential commitment and moved his family to Greensburg. My father wanted to move, buy a house, take the chance. My mother suspected Mr. Fink would not keep his word. "But then we could always move back," my father tried to reason. My mother held firm.

In the end, my father decided to give Mr. Fink an ultimatum—a guaranteed partnership or a guaranteed resignation. He had saved his money, and he was ready to start his own business. Mr. Fink chose the latter and suddenly my father was on his own. He selected a tiny, Catholic bedroom community in the Pittsburgh suburbs, Brookline, and started a family shoe store specializing in children's high quality and corrective footwear. It was called, in honor of his family, Tryson's—for three sons. The possibility of "Tri-son's," with an *i*, never appealed to him. It didn't look right on paper. Being an independent merchant, beholden to no one, turned out to be a wise move, for it isn't clear that Mr. Fink would have kept his promise or that my father could have held his blazing temper long enough to have been the recipient of Mr. Fink's largesse.

But the big question one might ask is: Why would my father name his beloved shoe store for his children, as if it were a point of pride? Not that he wasn't proud of having three sons; the concept of fathering, of planting or continuing the Gutkind seed obviously struck a comfortable chord. But what to do with the children he created and how to nurture them beyond naming a shoe store in their honor, never seemed to enter his mind. Did he believe that his sons could learn to live life properly by following in their father's footsteps, even though their father offered an unacceptable model of behavior to his children?

My father expected his sons to conduct themselves properly in every situation, whether or not he was involved, and, through some sort of imagined process of osmosis, to attribute their positive accomplishments to his non-existent counsel. Meanwhile, he was incapable of controlling our negative behavior or assuming the role of the family leader. As a father, he was a distant dictator; he turned his anger and frustration onto the people he loved most—his wife and his eldest son. He never vented any of his pent-up wrath on his sisters, Hattie and Ethel, who might have helped him more when he was growing up, but didn't—or his father himself. Jack refused to admit any wrongdoing from his father. "My dad did everything he could," he once said.

At the time he uttered those words, I thought he was also sending me a subtle message—that he had done everything he could for me, as a father, as I was growing up, that he had been basically a good father and had done his best. But I didn't reply, because I knew he hadn't done his best. Punching, strapping, and forcing your son into torturous isolation, as punishment, is not considered model behavior.

Facing a cash flow shortage in the mid-1970s, my father allowed part of his fire insurance to lapse. An arsonist set fire to the restaurant next door. My father's beloved shoe store, along with the restaurant, burned to the ground. That was the first time I remember feeling compassion for my father—and respect for his stoicism. He accepted his losses without whining, turned his back, and walked away.

The second time I felt a grudging compassion was fifteen years later. He was in the hospital with colon cancer. The doctors and my mother were in the corridor, discussing his poor prognosis and speculating about his death. I went into his room. My father looked up, engaging me eye-to-eye, a rare event, and nodded as if I knew exactly what he was about to say. Then he tilted his head, as if he was about to tell a story. Instead, he announced, "They think I am going to die. Can you imagine?" I didn't want him to die—and he didn't. But I was wondering if he was going to have some sort of epiphany about getting a second chance and becoming a better father. It was too late, though. I didn't need or want a better father now. My father should have worked much harder at fatherhood, if for no other reason than because he had been the orphan son.

My father's letter was his attempt to reach out and, perhaps, in a symbolic way, his reluctant apology. I understand how difficult this action might have been, but the fact is there is little he could do to make up for what happened when I was a kid. There is little he could do to make up for what happened when *he* was a kid, either. I suffered for the sins of his father and his stepmother. That's what I believe he was telling me in this letter. He wanted me to understand; I *did* understand, although understanding alone has not made his behavior more acceptable.

Now that I have become a father, my father is doing a good job healing my wounds by bonding with my son. Sometimes I watch him play with Sam in the living room of his old house and close my eyes, pretending that Sam is me, which, in many respects, he really is.

Yet, it makes me sad to think that I have known this man all my life—more than half a century—and I know little about him except for this abbreviated history. It's good that he wrote me a letter and supplied a chronology of his biographical points of reference. I appreciate it. But I haven't the slightest idea what he thinks about on a day-to-day basis and how he feels about the results of the nearly ninety years of his life. And because of our history of conflict and our lifelong lack of connection, I don't expect to ever find out. Which is not to say that I couldn't engage him in conversation about these matters, if I tried. But after so many years of distance and alienation, it doesn't seem worth the effort. I might find out something that would alter my entire perception of him and our relationship, and that scares me. As bad as I feel about my history with my father, I have decided that it is too late to change my mind about anything. I continue to play the cards that have been dealt me; I don't want another hand.

Mr. Meyers

In September 1966 I wandered into the Cathedral of Learning at the University of Pittsburgh, the massive forty-story monument to education, the tallest university classroom building in the United States, and registered for my first college course: Freshman English. The following evening, notebook and pencil in hand, I went to class.

Our teacher was a slender, pot-bellied, pockmarked man in his late twenties with a long nose and greasy black hair. Robert Meyers was a teaching assistant completing work on his Ph.D. in literature. I later learned that Meyers was married, had a couple of children, and that he had been offered a tenure-track position at a university somewhere in the Midwest, as soon as he was awarded his Ph.D., which was forthcoming in a few months. Mr. Meyers took our names, asked the appropriate questions, outlined his plan for the course and then, for the rest of the period, told us to write an essay he would critique and return the following week.

As I wrote this essay, about the beer-and-soda guys I had be-friended at Iggy's, I felt exhilarated. I had written book reports in high school, as well as a few essays for science and history classes. But this was fun—telling stories about my life. All awareness of time escaped me—until I looked up; I was the last person remaining in the classroom.

Sitting at a table in front of the class, I could tell that Mr. Meyers was getting antsy. He closed his book and exhaled sharply, smiling apologetically in my direction. Reluctantly, I ripped the pages from my notebook and handed the stack to him. It took me a couple of moments to pack up. Out of the corner of my eye, I could tell that

Mr. Meyers was reading what I had written. As I opened the door to depart, he said, "Wait." I went back into the room. "This is pretty good." He was pointing at my essay. "What do you do?" he asked. "I mean, in life. Or what do you want to do?"

I told him that this was why I decided to start college: to build a life and find a profession. I was lost, I admitted.

"Well," he motioned at my essay, pausing to nod and purse his lips, "This is pretty good. Well written. You ought to think about being a writer."

When Meyers suggested writing as a career, I was exhilarated—the first time anyone had offered career direction that made life hopeful or exciting or unique. Despite the fact that I had never achieved a grade higher than C in math, my high-school guidance counselor had recommended I become an accountant. This made no sense. Numbers made me sleepy. Even today I have difficulty adding and subtracting—even with a calculator.

But Mr. Meyers' suggestion struck a chord. After all, I was reading all the time. My passion for stories helped me get through the U.S. Coast Guard and partially rehabilitate myself physically and intellectually.

"Okay," I replied, not knowing anything about a writer's world or what one did to make a living as a writer, except to tell stories and write, "I think I will."

My writing career started in the public relations world. I got a job working for an agency as an assistant account executive, promoting carpet, cement mixers, a theater in the round and other small businesses. Success came quickly and I was awarded a special account: the Helium Centennial Committee for Government and Industry—an organization founded to celebrate the hundredth anniversary of the discovery of the element helium.

The cornerstone event was the creation of a monument in the middle of the biggest slum area in Amarillo, Texas, where helium was discovered, called the Helium Centennial Time Columns: four stainless steel time capsules, three on the bottom, coming together like a tripod, and a fourth intersecting in the middle and shooting straight up, six stories into the sky—a dramatic, erect penislike shaft glittering in the relentless southwest Texas sun. The event devised to inaugurate the time columns—a $1 million investment when adjusted for inflation—began when four helicopters lifted the corners of a gigantic black tarpaulin, hovered above the site and dropped the tarp over the entire monument, thus concealing it from view. The corners of the tarpaulin were securely anchored.

The day before the official inauguration, dozens of large helium-filled weather balloons were attached to the tarp, end-to-end. Senators, congressmen, and government bigwigs came from all across the country. The airport was mobbed. Every visitor was personally welcomed by the Amarillo Greeting Club: two rows of twelve cowboys in red gabardine pants, white shirts, blue bandanas, white gloves and hats, lined up like toy soldiers in front of the exit doors waiting to shake every visitor's hand and thank each of them for coming to Amarillo, which is what they said: "Welcome to Amarillo. Thanks for coming to Amarillo. Welcome to Amarillo. Thanks for coming to Amarillo. Welcome to Amarillo. Thanks for coming to Amarillo," twenty-four times.

The inaugural ceremonies featured high school bands playing the national anthem, the state anthem, and "The Yellow Rose of Texas." TV cameras from the three networks were represented. At the dot of noon, burley cowboys stationed at the corners where the tarpaulin had been anchored swung their axes. The ropes were severed. With music playing and cameras rolling, the balloons began rising, first slowly but then ever faster, climbing higher into the sky, until the tarp was lifted and the Helium Centennial Time Columns were dramatically revealed. The crowd hooted and hollered, then settled in for beer and barbecue, baked beans and Texas toast.

Down the road from the festivities were houses without plumbing and children playing in mud puddles in the middle of unpaved streets—a reality I subconsciously protested in a news release I wrote, which should have started with the following sentence: "People from throughout the country will have the opportunity to achieve immortality by nominating items to be included in the Helium Centennial Time Columns." Only after the release was sent to hundreds of newspapers, radio, and TV stations, nationwide, did I realize that I had omitted the *t* from the word *immortality*, an honest mistake I have never regretted.

I quit my job and, on my own, started writing essays and articles, often about eccentric, somewhat edgy subjects in which I could be an active participant, such as clowning for Ringling Brothers, wrangling at a rodeo, transcontinental trucking. I profiled a one-armed blacksmith, a cooper who practiced his craft in the old way with a *schnitzelbank* (a "shaving bench" or "shaving horse"), sparred with professional wrestling's heavyweight champion, Bruno Sammartino, and hunted rattlesnakes with a mountain man named McCool. Once, in the hills of eastern Kentucky, I joined a group called Judo and Karate for Christ, which chopped, kicked, flipped, and hurled fellow disciples in the name of the Lord Jesus.

As part of my research—I was working on an article for *Sports Illustrated Magazine*—I was initiated as a full-fledged Judo and Karate for Christ church member. This took place in a makeshift chapel— a spacious tent erected in the middle of a baseball field. I stood on the podium and cradled in my arms a large watermelon wedged between my crotch and chin, which I squeezed tightly into my stomach. At the count of three—and in the hush of the tent—the founder of the sect, Mike Crain, a black-belt karatist priest, blindfolded himself. Then one of his associates placed in Crain's hands a silver Samurai sword. Crain slowly and dramatically turned to me.

"Are you ready?" he asked.

"I'm ready," I said.

"Louder," he shouted. "The congregation must witness your sacrifice."

"I'm ready," I said, more loudly. But I was becoming less ready. What did he mean by sacrifice, I wondered?

"I can't hear you," Crain hollered.

"We can't hear you," the people echoed. There must have been two hundred men and women packed together on folding chairs in this tent, drinking iced tea and swatting the flies away with their Bibles.

"I am ready," I shouted.

"Do you believe?" Crain asked, at the top of his lungs and with a lilting chant, while lifting the Samurai sword, glittering in the colored lights of the tabernacle, high over his head.

"I believe," I said. I was lying, of course. The only thing I believed at that moment was that I was going to die. Besides, I was Jewish.

"Do you believe?" Crain asked one more time.

"I believe," I shrieked. Crain rose up on his toes and stretched himself backwards so that the back of the blade paralleled the back of his thighs. Then suddenly, ferociously, accompanied by an ear-piercing shout, he swung the gleaming sword down, down, down into the watermelon, severing it in half, so that the point of the blade swept narrowly past my chin, neck, chest, my stomach. I can feel it even now—a shocking awareness of the intimacy of that gliding slice of mutilation and death so close to my heart and to the end of my life. Then the severed watermelon fell from my hands and smashed into the floorboards of the podium, spilling its splendorous red juices down the stairs, puddling under the feet of the first-row congregates.

I regularly shared these true stories with my students at the University of Pittsburgh. I had begun teaching soon after earning my undergraduate degree and starting my first book (*Bike Fever*), about the motorcycle subculture and my travels through the country on two wheels and the people I interacted with. Real life is more bizarre and inspiring than anything that can be imagined—if you live through it—is what I told my students. This was the direction my writing was going and where my heart was—what others and I began calling "creative nonfiction."

Teeth

After breakfast, her husband looked up from across the table and announced that he was taking her into town to have all her teeth pulled out. It took a while for the meaning of his words to penetrate. Even when he said he was getting her a new set of teeth, she stared at him blankly. The memory of that morning nearly six months ago pained her even now.

"My teeth ain't perfect, but they never give me or my husband no trouble," she said, rolling her eyes and shaking her head back and forth slowly. "And suddenly, there he wanted to go and pull them all out. I've never been so surprised in all my life."

She was sitting on a stoop in front of the tarpaper-covered cabin in which she and her husband lived, petting the old coon dog, curled in a grimy heap at her feet, and watching the tractor-trailer trucks whoosh by. Each time a truck went up the road, she would wave and smile. The truckers would invariably wave back, as they roared by, bellowing smoke.

She told me that her loneliness was sometimes awful. It wasn't the mountains—she had lived here all her life and wasn't interested in anywhere else—but the fact that no one was around to talk to. The gloomy shadow that fell across her face blatantly telegraphed her desperation. Each time I visited, she went on and on, could hardly stop herself from talking and questioning me about my travels. She was enthralled by my motorcycle and the stories I told about Santa Fe, New Mexico; Amarillo, Texas; Pine Bluff, Arkansas—places far away from where she lived now. She wanted to see the world, which to her was anywhere beyond her own confining backyard.

The woman was a river of fat. Her body bulged and rippled in every direction, and her eyes, tucked into her pasty skin, looked like raisins pressed into cookie dough. Her hair was dirty gray, tangled and woolly, but you could tell her face had once been pretty. When she showed me her picture as an infant, I remarked that she looked like the Ivory Snow baby. Blushing, she covered her mouth and turned away. That was how we had first got on the subject of her teeth.

One day in town her husband was approached by the new dentist, a handsome young man in a white shirt and a blue-and-red-striped tie, who said his house needed a new roof. Would he be interested in installing it in return for money or services?

Her husband was a short, wiry old man of seventy-two, who resembled a chicken hawk, with a hooked nose and arms that bowed out like furled wings. He hunched forward when he walked, as if he were about to take off flying. He told the dentist he would think on it for a while.

That evening, after supper, he stooped down and peered into her mouth, testing each of her teeth with his thumb and forefinger to see how well they were rooted. "Smile," he told her. "Laugh." She followed his instructions to the letter, as was her habit. Over the next few days, he watched her every chance he got. It was early autumn when he finally went back into town to make the deal. She never knew anything about it.

The woman explained that she and her husband had very little use for cash, bartering for almost everything they needed. They traded vegetables, cultivated on their tiny patch of land, for fruit—corn for peaches, tomatoes for apples, pickles for pears, beets for pretty "blue-fire" plums. He chopped wood in return for mason jars. Periodically, he repaired a car for a guy who owned a dry goods store in town in exchange for clothes for both of them. By bartering instead of buying and selling, they hardly paid Uncle Sam a penny's worth of taxes.

Last summer, he raised a barn for some city folks, recently retired near here, in return for an old engine from a '64 Buick and a side of beef. The engine went into a pickup truck they had gotten for 150 dozen eggs. Paid out over a period of three months, the eggs came from their chicken coops out back. The pickup was then swapped to the owner of a local filling station for credit for two hundred gallons of gas, plus an assortment of parts and tools. Meanwhile, she boiled up the beef on the old black cast-iron stove that had belonged to his grandfather and canned and stored most of it in the cold-cellar cave under the house. She cut the remainder of the beef in strips and hung them like wet socks above the stove, smoking and shriveling them down to jerky. From the spring to the fall, her husband went fishing each evening after dinner. When he collected a big batch of trout, she stewed them in the pressure cooker until the whole fish, bones and all, was white and meaty like tuna. This was what they would eat next winter and the winters thereafter. Their cave was stocked with years of stuff.

Her husband never talked about his work and what was owed to him in the way of goods and services, and she never asked. Despite her significant contribution, the actual swapping wasn't her business. Years ago, her daddy had told her in no uncertain terms exactly what she needed to know to get herself through life. He was a man much like her husband, didn't owe anyone and never wasted anything. No words were wasted in conversation, unless some specific point was to be made. Otherwise, silence was golden.

One night, however, her father came outside and squeezed down on the stoop beside her. They lived in an old house along the side of the road, about the same size as the one in which she and her husband lived now. But her father only rented it for fifty dollars a month. Neither her father nor his father before him had ever owned a piece of property straight out.

At the time, she didn't know that the old man was dying from cancer. Her mother had also died from cancer, and she had had to quit school in the sixth grade to take care of the rest of the kids and keep house. Recently, her two older brothers had joined the army, while the younger kids were sent to foster homes. Now, she and her father were home alone. She was fifteen at the time.

They sat side by side as the night grew colder. The moon shimmered in the glittering dish of sky, but the air felt like rain. Suddenly he cleared his throat. The sound of his voice made her feel uncomfortable, similar to how she felt trying on a new pair of boots.

"What else is there in life?" He said this as if in summation after a long conversation, which she had somehow missed. Then he paused. She would never forget his face as they sat there. His hard, sharp features seemed to disintegrate in the darkness. The glitter reflecting from the moonlight faded from the blue of his eyes.

"You work to eat, you eat to live, you live to work." He sighed. "That's all there are to it."

That philosophy repelled me and was the reason I was not ever going to be happy shoe-dogging with my father or staying around Pittsburgh making a life with the likes of Steve Mayerstein and Melvin Herwald—any of that old crowd from school. I didn't know, exactly, what was ahead of me when I first got on a motorcycle— I certainly had little confidence I could make it as a writer—but anything was better than limiting my life plan to mere survival and maintaining the status quo, which was so uninspiring.

But this woman's notions of escape were too vague to be transformed into a reality. She lacked direction—and a concrete dream. Robert Meyers had anchored my possibilities. Gave me permission to try to turn my dreams of a different and better life into reality by verbalizing what I had been hereto afraid to even imagine. I wouldn't be here, on my big, black R-60 BMW road warrior, living this life from one end of the country to the other, without that vital exchange between teacher and student.

The next morning, the man who was soon to become her husband made himself known. Miraculously, all of the details had been worked out between the man and her father in advance, without her having the slightest idea of what was happening. The following afternoon, the man came and took her away. Two weeks later, her father died.

She cleared her throat and motioned toward the house with her fat, flesh-soaked arm. "We came right here to these two acres and moved into an old shed out back. It ain't there no more. Tore it down to salvage the wood for this place. First we made sure we had good water, then we started building. From start to finish it took two years to get all set up. The winters were awful, but the summers weren't too bad."

All this happened some thirty years ago. Her husband had been married once before. His first wife died or left him, she wasn't sure, and his children, whom she never met, were all grown up and living somewhere in another part of the state. Once in a great while, there was a letter, which he would read carefully, his lips moving, then stuff into his pocket, shaking his head and muttering. He would go on, muttering and cursing, shaking his head, for days at a time, without so much as an explanation.

Her own brothers and sisters all lived near here, but hardly ever stopped by or invited her to visit. Like most everyone else, they were more than a little afraid of her somber, silent husband.

Once again, she paused to wave at a trucker, barreling up the narrow two-lane highway. Their shack had been built unusually close to the asphalt. Even from up in the sleeping loft inside, you could hear the cinders and feel the wind when the trucks rumbled by. She said she was so shocked and angry when she found out about the deal her husband had made with the new dentist that she started screaming and yelling. "I had never acted that way before, but I just couldn't help myself. All of a sudden, I went crazy. My husband didn't know what to do."

He had turned away, glaring in silence out the window. It was still early. The sun was just beginning its ascent up the hill toward them. His eyes narrowed. Time passed as he stared down the road. His brows, thick and hairy, cast a shadow, like umbrellas over his eyelids. When the sunlight reached up as far as their house, he got up and finished dressing. He bit off a plug of tobacco, stuffed it under his cheek, put on his old grimy baseball cap, climbed into his pickup, and turned her over. When he saw his wife come out onto the porch, he threw the truck into reverse, backed up, and leaned out the window. He wanted to have his say one more time. "We shook hands on a new set of teeth. It's owed to me."

She turned and walked back into the house without a word. He peeled out onto the asphalt, his tires spitting gravel.

In no time, her best clothes were out of the drawer and piled on the bed. She found an old suitcase, cleaned it inside and out carefully before laying in her clothes. The last time she had been on any sort of trip was when her husband had come to take her from her daddy. They didn't have a suitcase then. All her possessions, including her mother's big black roasting pan, fit easily into a medium-sized cardboard box. Her father carried the box down to the road and they waited together until the man who was to become her husband arrived. The whole thing—packing, waiting, and driving away—all took about ten minutes. It went by in a blur, one moment stacked up on top of another.

Thinking back, she realized that her life had ended right about then. She had been isolated with this man who hardly talked to her and whom she hardly knew, a man who had refused to discuss his past for over thirty years. At least with her father there was evidence of some roots and another life somewhere behind the one he had been living. But this man's world was bleak, both behind and beyond. He offered little more than a nod or a grunt for sustenance each day. Her father's words, uttered with such sadness and resignation on that damp, dark night so many centuries ago, came back to her now. You work to eat, you eat to live, you live to work. That's all there are to it.

All right. She had lived her life in accordance with her father's wishes, had never asked for anything from anyone, never shirked her responsibilities or wasted a breath. She had always done whatever her husband had told her to do—and more. But giving up a part of her own body simply for the sake of a business deal was too much. It was going too far. A person has a God-given right to own certain things, especially when they were born with them.

The last thing she did before leaving was to go out to the pump house and peer into the mirror. The image she saw glaring back at her was awful. She was too old, too fat, and too dirty. But, if anything, her face had held up best of all. There was still a spark, a hint of the beauty that might have been.

Her daddy, who never had more than a dollar in his pocket at any one time, had always bragged that the Good Lord had made him rich by blessing him with a daughter with a million-dollar smile. Even now, she could hear the distant echo of his praise. She wasn't going to let that damn bastard she married squash the memory by pulling out her teeth.

She looked up at me. The shroud that had fallen over her face as she told her story momentarily lifted. "Used to be my husband would leave me alone from early morning until supper. But now, things is different. He's liable to ride by anytime, just to check and see if I'm still here. Sometimes I hide out behind the chicken coops and wait for him. When the house looks empty, he'll stop to see where I am. He always pretends he's come back for tools or materials, but I know I got him worried. It serves him right."

She dug her fingers into her scalp, shook her head vehemently, scratching simultaneously before continuing. "I left the house that morning, hitchhiked into town, and bought a ticket for Davenport, Iowa. Davenport was the only city in the state I could think of. My daddy traveled all over the country when he was younger. He told me you could drive for half a day in any one direction in Iowa and not see anything else but a green carpet of corn, just bending and stretching in the distance."

She pushed her big blubbery legs out into the grass, right near where the old coon dog was lying. Once in a while, the dog would thrash around and thump its tail against the ground. A couple of times, it pushed itself up and crawled over on top of us. The woman had on brown double-knit slacks worn through at the knees. Her blouse was white with alternating pink and blue pastel stripes, although the colors were graying from repeated washings. This was the outfit she wore as she climbed aboard the bus and headed toward Davenport. Her clothes looked a lot better back then, she said.

It took nearly three hours to get to Pittsburgh, where they stopped and idled in the depot for about forty-five minutes. She did not get off the bus. They stopped twice on the highway in Ohio and once more in Indiana, but she remained in her seat, guarding her suitcase.

"I tell you, I've never done so much thinking in my entire life as

I did on that bus, looking through the window, reading the neon signs and watching the headlights from the cars. Most of the people around me were sleeping, and none of them were too friendly. Not that I tried to do much talking. To tell the truth, I was scared half to death."

She wasn't actually thinking, she explained, as much as she was dreaming —with her eyes open. Her window was like an imaginary TV screen, and she could see the images of her past reflected before her. She saw her father carrying the cardboard box down to the side of the road. As the cancer took its toll, he had shriveled up like an old root. Then she saw the man who was to be her husband pull up. He put the cardboard box into the bed of the truck, opened up the passenger door, and helped her inside.

"I remember looking right into his face as he done this, the first time I had ever looked him full in the face. And then, as I sat in the darkness on that bus, I pictured how he looked earlier that morning when he leaned across the table and told me he was going to take away my teeth. And you know what? He was the same. Those thirty years we had spent together had bloated me like a balloon and wrecked up my face but, except for a little more gray in his whiskers, that bastard ain't changed one bit."

She paused, shook her head, chuckled, then shook her head again and again. It wasn't easy to suddenly accept the reality of what had happened. The shiny sadness of her life reflected in her eyes.

I looked away, down behind the tarpaper shack toward the outhouse across the field. It had a three-hole bench. There were four or five old cars dumped into a gully behind the outhouse and an abandoned windowless school bus, teetering on the edge.

"I never made it to Davenport," she said, after a while. "But I got all the way to Chicago. You ever been to the bus station in Chicago? More people there than I ever seen, all in one place. Half of them don't speak English, and none of them was white. The moment I got off that bus, seeing all them colored and hearing all that foreign commotion, I was completely confused. I was hungry, but didn't want to spend any money. I also wanted to clean up a little, but with all them people, I was afraid to make a decision."

After a while, she found herself a bench back in the corner, out of the way, and sat down to try to think things out. She still had her ticket to Davenport, Iowa, but didn't particularly want to go there any more. She didn't want to go anywhere, as a matter of fact. She wasn't willing to move one inch from where she was. She must have dozed off, for the next thing she remembered was feeling a hand on her shoulder, shaking her gently. Someone was saying her name. No one would know her name in Chicago, so maybe she really was back home, about to emerge from a terrible dream.

But when she finally opened her eyes, an elderly man with horn-rimmed glasses and a tiny, pinched nose introduced himself as a representative of the Traveler's Aid Society, whatever that was. The man's voice was soft and reassuring. As he talked, he picked up her bag, wrapped his arm around her ample shoulders, helped her up, and led her across the bus station.

When her husband had discovered her missing, the man explained, he had contacted their minister, who somehow traced her to Pittsburgh and subsequently to Chicago. There was also a Traveler's Aid representative waiting at the Davenport bus station, just in case she had made it that far.

They were moving at a brisk pace, passing the ticket counters and neatly wending their way through the milling crowd. She felt like a piece of livestock. "Where are you taking me?"

"There's a bus to Pittsburgh leaving in about ten minutes. Your husband already wired the money." He smiled and continued to talk to her in his quiet and reassuring manner, as they pushed through a big set of swinging doors and headed on down a broad cement runway toward a long line of idling buses. Drivers in neatly pressed gray uniforms stood by the doors of their respective vehicles, puffing cigarettes and punching tickets, as she and the man hurried by.

"But I already have a ticket to Davenport, Iowa."

"You can cash it in when you get back home . . ." He paused, all the while continuing to lead her down along the row of buses. "Of course, I can't force you to do anything you don't want to do." He shrugged and smiled apologetically. "I can't even help you make up your mind."

By this time, they were approaching the bus to Pittsburgh. She felt his hand on her back, urging her gently toward the bus. He handed a ticket and her suitcase to the driver.

Meanwhile, she hesitated, momentarily resisting the pressure on her back. She tried desperately to think things out, but her mind was blank, as was her future.

With nothing better to do, she walked up the steps, dropped into a seat by the window, and closed her eyes. She did not allow herself to open her eyes until hours later, when the bus pulled into Pittsburgh. She was so confused and embarrassed, she had completely forgotten to say goodbye to the man with the horn-rimmed glasses who had helped her.

Now she looked up at me, smiling and winking. "My husband came to meet me." The thought evidently amused her, for she shook her head back and forth, chuckling. "On the way home, we talked things over, got everything out in the open for the very first time. I told him how lonely I was, how it wasn't fair the way he constantly mistreated me. I said that I should be consulted in his decisions about how we spend our money. I told him that I didn't have enough clothes, that I wanted to go into town more often, and that, because he was such a damn hermit, I didn't have no friends or family." She nodded emphatically. "I let him have it with both barrels. He had never allowed no one to talk to him that way before in his entire life."

I stood up. More than two hours had passed since we had first started talking. The sky was clouding over. In this part of western Pennsylvania, rain erupts suddenly, swallowing the hillsides and ravaging the roads. Besides, I was getting cold, sitting so long on that stoop. And my pants were filthy, where the old coon dog had tracked mud all over me. I walked briskly back to my motorcycle.

"He tries to be nice," she said, as she followed along behind me. "But you really can't change him. You couldn't ever change my daddy either," she added. "When you come right down to it, they was both dark and silent men."

I nodded, pulled on my helmet and kicked down on the starter. The machine cranked to life as I straddled the seat. From past experience, I knew that I couldn't wait for the right moment to leave. Otherwise, I'd be waiting forever. I had to depart even while she was still in the act of talking.

She planted her foot in my path and grabbed my arm. "You know, he drove by two or three times while we was sitting here talking. He'll want to know who you are and everything that was said. Hell," she said, smiling and winking, finally stepping out of the way, so that I could pull out, "I ain't telling him nothing. It serves him right."

The woman prepared herself extra special for her husband's homecoming that evening.

She went into the pump house and sponged herself down from head to toe, ran a brush through her hair a hundred times, scrubbed the grime from her fingers until the half-moons of her nails were white. Back in the house, in the loft where they slept, she got out the nice green cotton jumper-dress with the pretty yellow and white floral design and laid it out on the quilt. He had bought her the dress the day she came home. She had only taken it out of the box once, the following Sunday when they went to church.

After preparing dinner and setting the table nice and neat, she went back upstairs and put on the dress. Then she dusted herself with some fancy-smelling powder she had ordered through a magazine and gotten in the mail. She was just about ready, when his truck crackled outside on the gravel. He walked into the house. She could hear him move about downstairs, looking into the big pot on the cast-iron stove, sniffing what was for dinner. But not until he walked across the room and started up the ladder toward the loft, did she reach into the water glass on the nightstand beside their bed. Only then did she put in her new teeth.

Dog Story

In my early thirties during the waning days of my first marriage, I experienced true love for the first time. He was a mostly black, smallish German shepherd with frosty white trimmings, named Icy, whom I had raised from a tiny puppy and who spent the days with me in my office as I wrote. We took walks together in the evening, went to the park on weekends to play and run.

When my first wife and I were divorced, however, Icy, whom I had obedience-trained and who had been awarded many blue ribbons for excellence in obedience trials, went over the edge, becoming unpredictable and often hostile to strangers. Once, sitting at my side on the street as I talked with a friend, he suddenly leaped at her four-year-old son and lifted a chunk of skin from the fleshy part of his cheek directly below his eyes. A quarter-inch upward and the boy could have been blinded.

Friends urged me to put Icy to sleep, insisting that a dog exhibiting such frightening and hostile behavior has crossed over a line into a no-man's land from which, for an animal, there is usually no return. But I held on to Icy for months, despite his attack and his hostile threatening behavior to other guests. My personal situation was pretty dismal and Icy was not only my best friend, but also the last vestige of my six-year marriage, a symbol and a connection I did not want to release. But the day I came home and found him chewing on the ankle of a friend who had come to visit and saw the surprise and terror in my friend's eyes, I realized that enough was enough.

I contacted the captain of the local police K-9 corps, who, accompanied by a young officer in search of a canine partner, arrived at my house the following afternoon. They watched through the kitchen window while I took Icy out into the backyard and put him through his paces. It was a perfect performance. Icy would sit, heel, lie down, fetch, and come in response to either voice commands or hand signals. After a while, the captain came out onto the back porch: "Yes, we'll take him," he said. "But we want him right now."

"I hadn't planned on giving him up so soon," I said, panicking. "I just wanted you to meet him."

"In our experience in these cases, the best thing is for us to take your dog away before you think too much about it."

This advice seemed logical. And I couldn't think of an alternative solution. I handed the leash to the young officer, turned my back and walked to the front window to watch them depart. My last memory of Icy was when he paused at the back of the police van and turned toward me with a look of surprise and abandonment I will never forget, as if to say, "You are letting them take me away? How could you?" I knew that my answer was "How could I not?"

Some months after Icy's departure in the K-9 van, I received a phone call from the secretary of the precinct to which Icy and his police officer partner had been assigned. She explained that Icy had attacked the officer's children—K-9 dogs will usually live at home with their human partners—and had become increasingly unreliable. Tomorrow, the officer was driving him to the country to be introduced to an elderly man on a small farm where he might find a home as a guard dog. If the man was not interested, Icy would be euthanized. She was calling to say that I could have Icy back if I wanted, however, and subsequently make the decision about Icy's fate on my own.

I missed Icy, would have enjoyed having him back—the old Icy that is—and I felt somewhat responsible for the change in his nature. But my guilt for what happened was not reason enough to bring this angry dog that hurt little children back to my new home. I could not, on the other hand, let Icy go without one last look. The following morning I got up early and drove to the police officer's house to wait surreptitiously for him to transport Icy to the country. I caught sight of him in his family car with Icy sitting in the back seat peering out of the rear window. Instinctively, I began to follow.

About forty minutes later, the officer turned off the highway onto a narrow, isolated blacktop road and then pulled into a dirt driveway in front of a small frame farmhouse. I drove to the top of a hill where I could watch the comings and goings at the house while the officer led Icy on a leash onto the porch. I finally caught a clear glimpse of Icy, who seemed a bit more filled-out than I remembered him, but fit and healthy. The old man was short, skinny, and scraggly. The police officer did most of the talking, periodically pointing down at Icy and petting him, with the old man nodding warily. It wasn't hard to know, judging by their body language, that the conversation was not going in Icy's favor. Within a few minutes, the visit was over. The two men shook hands cursorily.

The officer then drove into a nearby town, down the main street, turning off onto a side road and stopping in front of a small veterinary hospital. In retrospect, I should have known exactly what was happening as soon as Icy and the police officer stopped at the veterinarian's office, but I sat in my car across the street, theorizing that the farmer had insisted that Icy undergo a physical examination before accepting him on the farm. I didn't become fully aware that something else was happening until the police officer emerged from the veterinarian's office, got into his car, and drove away—alone.

I jumped out of my car and dashed into the veterinary office. An elderly woman at a small reception desk looked up and smiled. I asked to see the doctor. Before she could answer, I could hear in the background Icy's unmistakable bark—but not the friendly barking I remembered so clearly as he excitedly greeted me each time I came home, a happy welcome I would never forget. The tone and timbre were different; it was an angry, snarling sound. The woman informed me that the doctor was busy. I said that I would come back later. I left the office and followed the sound to the rear of the building and peeked inside an open window.

For an instant I saw Icy, my same wonderful beautiful black dog with the frosted paws and eyebrows, but a glimpse into his angry, frantic eyes convinced me that he was also very different from the dog I loved. Something had happened to Icy over that year— something I witnessed starting to happen the months prior to his departure from my life. He had lost his center, his stability, his awareness of right and wrong.

Veterinarians lack a basic understanding of why this condition in animals comes about, but it is almost always disseminated by thoughtless and one-dimensional breeding practices. This I learned when I researched my book, *The Veterinarian's Touch*, inspired by Icy. Too much emphasis is placed on physical conformation by owners and breeders at the expense of temperament—thereby per- petuating unsound mental traits in certain breeds of dogs. At the same time, the entire breed can suffer great prejudice, such as in the case of German shepherds, although the vast majority of this breed possesses a basically harmless temperament. The aggression displayed by these dogs is often fear-related, sparked by cruelty and mistreatment. Mental or behavioral disturbances suffered by animals are probably not dissimilar from the quirks in the human mind that cause a perfectly settled and sane man or woman to suddenly, without a clear and discernible reason, lose touch with reality.

When this happens, we cannot euthanize human beings, but because animals are subservient in this society to humans and considered to be property, owners possess the right of disposal. Veterinarians consider euthanasia both a burden and a great luxury, in that they possess the capability of saving a patient (and family) from seemingly endless agony and pain. I didn't like the idea of euthanizing Icy, which is exactly what the veterinarian was in the process of doing, but in retrospect, I think I understood it.

Euthanasia is often difficult for human beings to accept because many people tend to be very anthropomorphic about animals and to assume that the threat or realization of loss of life means the same thing to an animal as it does to a human being. People who know animals will tell you that animals experience fear and pain, just like humans, and they will display the same general range of symptoms, as a human would show in similar physical circumstances. But they don't worry about losing their lives and they do not fear or conceive of death. At that point at which the euthanasia occurs, animals close their eyes and go to sleep as they do every day or night, without a preconceived notion or expectation of waking up the following morning.

This is one of the reasons why veterinarians are veterinarians: People are much more difficult to deal with, and animals are so accepting and more often so very responsive to the work of a veterinarian. Even when animals are vicious, veterinarians don't often display animosity. "You don't hate the animal," one veterinarian told me, "you simply fear it. And you know that they're hostile or aggressive for a reason. And the reasons are usually better than human reasons." Animals do not display racial prejudice; they don't have ulterior motives. It's always a functional thing. If they are being vicious to us, it's because they're afraid and they're trying to protect themselves or their owners. This is a quality to admire.

The playwright Eugene O'Neill was an avid animal lover who treated his pets with the kindness and regard he extended to people, but who also understood that dogs and cats were significantly different from human beings. In a story entitled "The Last Will and Testament of an Extremely Distinguished Dog," O'Neill wrote:

Dogs do not fear death as men do. We accept it as part of life, not as something alien and terrible, which destroys life. What may come after death, who knows? I would like to believe . . . that there is a Paradise where one is always young and full-bladdered; where all the day one dillies and dallies with a continuous multitude of houris, beautifully spotted; where jack rabbits that run fast but not too fast (like the houris) are as the sands of the desert; where each blissful hour is mealtime; where in long evenings there are a million fireplaces with logs forever burning, and one curls himself up and blinks into the flames and nods and dreams, remembering the old brave days on earth, and the love of one's Master and Mistress.

O'Neill's empathy helped me understand and accept what Icy might next experience, although at the time of this incident, I was nearly overwhelmed with a surge of remorse and guilt that almost triggered a daring intervention; my fantasy was to dive through the window, scoop Icy off the floor and run away with him. But I realized that the damage had been done; Icy and I would not live happily every after. A rescue would simply complicate my life and mislead Icy. He would have to be put to sleep eventually. The veterinarian was an older man, perhaps in his late sixties, slender and balding, and had obviously performed this very same act of mercy hundreds of times. He approached Icy with a quiet tenderness and a soothing, sensitive voice that calmed the angry dog. His tenderness calmed me, too. Icy sniffed at the veterinarian's fingers before permitting the man to pet him gently and soothingly. Icy began to whimper. I don't think he was aware of what was about to happen to him, but I do imagine that he felt a momentary sense of rest. The hypodermic needle suddenly appeared in the veterinarian's hand, and almost immediately, Icy slipped soundlessly to the linoleum.

When I returned home later that day, I sat down in the room I used as an office. A photo of Icy, his white-tipped paw resting on his favorite toy, a basketball, which he had endlessly pushed and chased around our backyard, was above my desk. I sat for a while and thought about the fun I had had with Icy and the loyalty he had displayed through all of our years together—considerably more loyalty than my first wife, who had cheated on me and eventually moved in with a man she met at the Greek Food Festival. The fact that my marriage was at an end paled when compared with the way in which my wife took her leave, in the dark of night, when I was hundreds of miles away, helpless, like when Patsy Guttman disappeared with Steve Mayerstein at my high school prom and I searched the dance floor, an island alone in a sea of groping lovers.

But the difference between then and now was my double image. When Patsy had abandoned me for Mayerstein, I was fat; now I wasn't—or least part of me wasn't fat. That "fall down nine times get up ten" part of me was increasingly becoming the real me—not the blob of the bar mitzvah boy who wilted in the perspiring oblivion of his forty-four husky suit self-image.

Clarity

I was in the Georgetown Inn in Washington DC one steamy summer evening when a power failure occurred. The lights went out just as I was in the process of telephoning home—we hadn't actually made contact. The television went black. The hum of the air conditioner stopped. The phone was dead.

Peering out the window, the only illumination I could see was from car headlights. People were streaming out of the stores and restaurants and into the streets, shadowy and anonymous from where I stood. Unhappy about being confined to a darkened hotel room and curious about what was happening down below—what I might be missing—I rushed down five flights, through the pitch-black lobby and out into the street to join them.

By this time, most people seemed to assume that the blackout would go on for a while. This wasn't to be a quick fix. Radio reports highlighted the downed power lines; a fire at a power station had been caused by a freak electrical storm. The streets were teeming with people, some like me wandering aimlessly, unsure about where to go and what to do, while others were pushing through the mass of sweaty bodies trying to escape the area.

Traffic was horrendous, but police cars and vans slowly began to appear, barricading side roads with their cars and with makeshift sawhorses so that traffic could only flow on the main roads. People could enter Georgetown by walking, only. Uniformed officers, nightsticks in hand, positioned themselves on every street corner. Owners and employees of shops, holding brooms, hammers, and baseball bats, were standing at the storefronts of their businesses. The mass of people combined with the heat, so intense that it baked into my body from the sidewalk and the soles of my shoes upward into my boiling scalp, created an atmosphere of defensiveness and hostility. "Get the fuck out of here," a man standing in front of a small jewelry-gift shop told me when a passerby pushed me into him.

"Sorry man," I said. "It wasn't my fault."

"You want some of this?" the man said, producing a baseball bat that had been concealed behind his back and waving it threateningly.

"What're you, crazy?" I said. "Calm down."

A policeman came up and positioned himself behind me. "What's the problem?" he said. "Do you have any business here? This store is closed, you know?"

"Look," I tried to explain. "I was pushed in this direction—I didn't want to go here. And I accidentally bumped this guy. Now he is threatening me with a baseball bat."

"I told him to get the fuck out of here," the man with the baseball bat said. "He has no business here."

"Do you have business on this street?" the policeman said again.

"I'm staying at the Georgetown Inn," I said.

"That's not business," said the man with the baseball bat. "That's pleasure."

"There's no pleasure sitting in the heat and sweating in the dark," I said.

"Now you are getting wise." The man took a step toward me, lifted the bat behind his head and began making threatening motions with his wrists. "I'll light up your night. You'll see stars."

For an instant, my temper flared. I had seen a lot of unwelcome and painful stars over the past week, and I was in no mood to be intimidated by a crazed bully, even if he did have a baseball bat and even though a policeman was breathing down my neck. I hadn't done anything to this man; I had only tried to take a little walk and clear my head. Which is why I had come to Washington in the first place—for a meeting I really did not have to attend—to clear my head and try to understand what was happening in my life and what to do about it.

I was not a person to run away from pressing matters—or from people threatening me—but over the years I had learned that clarity often comes with distance—a disconnection from the troubles that haunt me. The significant transitions in my life—from ne'er-do-well to serious student and later from motorcycle wanderer to committed writer—had been precipitated by a reasoned and purposeful evacuation for a measured period of time from the source of trauma or ambivalence.

In this case, it was from my family—my wife, specifically, my second wife—who had ambushed me a week ago by telling me that she wanted me to leave our house and that she wanted—*we needed*—to get divorced. It was a joke, the *we-needed-to-get-divorced* part, although I was not laughing, and to me it was not funny. *She* suddenly needed to—was obsessed with divorce. I, on the other hand, felt that it was incumbent upon us to work things out.

Not that I had been unaware that our marriage was in jeopardy; but we had been seeing a therapist for nearly a year, a kind, elderly, patient man who had helped us understand and release our anger and animosity toward one another in a safe and controlled manner. I had thought for sure that we were making progress. My wife even said so, repeatedly, to me and to the therapist, that she was feeling better about our relationship; our friendship was returning. But clarity had come to her when I was least expecting it, so it seemed.

"Is there any reason for you to be walking the streets?" the policeman asked, stepping between me and the man with the baseball bat.

"Not really; I'm just looking around."

"If I were you," said the policeman, "I'd look somewhere else."

Even though I felt I was in the right—I hadn't done anything and there was no reason to suspect that I was a potential looter—I realized that the policeman's instincts were correct—it was time to get me away from that man, or get us away from one another, because we were both rather edgy and ready to erupt.

I hadn't done anything to my wife, either, and there was no reason to suspect that I would cause her any harm or trouble, I thought, as I wandered back to the hotel. While it was true that there were two sides to every story and that I was not an easy person to live with, she knew that I loved her, that I had been a faithful husband and supportive friend. She wasn't denying this. I wanted to try to work on our marriage and nurse it back toward our original level of comfort—when we both loved and desired one another—a starting point from which we might nurture new levels of understanding and friendship, I told her. That sounds idealistic. But actually, I was being practical. We had a young son, Sam, just now entering kindergarten. This was the time to build the family— not break up the family.

"But you wanted your mother to leave your father," she frequently pointed out during our sessions with the fatherly therapist. "You were six years old and you were unhappy, remember?" Patricia is short and slight, and her voice rises to a rather unnatural falsetto when she is frightened or upset. Her eyes also give her away; they are frequently wide and wild looking, reflecting the instability of her moods and responses to the world, as on that day in the therapist's office.

"But I am not my father," I said. "It is not fair to lump us in together."

The moment the lights had died in my Georgetown hotel room, the memories of being incarcerated in the dark by my father when I was a child came flooding back, and I had been compelled to escape into the street. Even today, so many decades later, I often sleep with a radio or television on, so that I can hear voices and not feel so isolated and alone. "I resent your comparison of me and my father," I had told my wife. "I am not a lunatic and I do not terrify my son."

I thought back to a time, once, after my father had beaten me, when my mother took the car and drove me to the park, where we sat on a bench. I begged her to rescue me from my father's fury, to take me away, to find us a new life and me another father, but she refused. She said she had nowhere to go and no way to support me. She said a boy needed a father every day of his life, even if he was a bad father. "What would happen if the father I married was worse than the father you have?"

She was being untruthful, I knew, and to a certain extent manipulative. My mother could have gone home to her father and mother, and they would have taken care of both us until she could get a job or find a new husband; or we could have just stayed with them, forever. My grandparents were in good health and generally well off. I adored them.

But my mother was afraid of the humiliation of being alone and on her own; she preferred being with a bad man with the capacity for bursts of goodness than to be with no man at all, at least back then, in the 1950s, when it was decidedly more difficult to be a single woman, especially one without a college education or skilled profession.

My two younger brothers had not been born yet. And who could imagine, at that moment, as unhappy and helpless as we both were, my mother and me, that she would even further complicate her situation by agreeing to build our family with two more children? Years later, she told me that she wanted me to have siblings so that I would have company and support at home and not feel so all alone. "That was a terrible reason to have children," I told her. "Didn't you know that?" She looked away and changed the subject. We both knew that her refusal to answer was her answer.

"But you could be," Patricia had said while the kindly therapist listened. "You could turn into your father. You are the same blood, and you have the same temper. When you are angry, you are nearly out of control."

"Are you your mother?" I countered. "You could turn into your mother. Your temper is worse than mine."

"God forbid," she said.

Her mother was a demanding, nagging witch of a woman who had drained Patricia of self-esteem and made her feel fearful of the entire adult world. Trapped in a warp of arrested development, Patricia had never passed through a stage of emotional adolescence; when it came to interacting socially, she was always rebellious and angry. Wherever we went and whomever I introduced her to, people would inevitably ask: "Why won't your wife talk to me?" Or they would say, "I turned around and suddenly I saw her glaring. What's her problem?" Her problem was other people.

To Patricia, all other people were adult authority figures who were going to be mean and make her feel unworthy, as had her mother. People with more knowledge or money or degrees were automatically intimidating. I was the worst offender—her mother in a man's body—or so she imagined.

How and why I became so intricately involved with this woman has only recently become clear to me. Long before I realized that I needed to have a family, I had actually become a parent—Patricia's. I guided, pushed, and prodded her to achieve her secret goal, which was a college degree. Patricia, an LPN (licensed practical nurse) had had a history of starting school, taking a few courses and doing well—until something especially challenging, such as algebra or statistics, or a demanding (and demeaning) professor confronted her—and then she would drop out.

Patricia never begged me to help her get through school. She would never expose herself to rejection by actually asking for help. But she suffered loudly, emotionally, with plunging bouts of depression. As her friend and periodic lover, I saw it as my duty to rescue her from her agonizing shroud of despair. Thus I relentlessly drove her forward to achieve what she considered unobtainable in the same way I drove myself all my life based on the lessons I had learned in the military and in all of my writing and research experiences. With enough hard work and with an unwavering dedication, a person could, sooner or later, achieve virtually any goal if they wanted it badly enough. But my motto—"Fall down nine times and get up ten"—drove her crazy. It reminded her of her mother's constant pushing and nagging.

"Tell me that one more time, and I will kill you," she often told me—and she meant it.

But I persisted, anyway—especially in therapy. "So we're not the perfect couple; we both have our baggage, and we have significant problems with one another but does that mean separation and divorce? Why quit?"

"We do what we have to do," she said.

"Aren't we stronger than that?" I persisted again. "We could work together and change. Never give up," I added. This would irritate her even more.

"It takes a lot of strength to do what I am doing, too," she said. "I want to change; I am already changing—without you."

I do not believe that my mother was being brave and heroic by returning to my father—she was fearful and to a certain extent cowardly—but she was also doing the right thing, from her own point of view. She displayed her own strength of endurance by managing and somehow moderating the ever-increasing friction between my father and me and the outbursts of rage that sent the household and sometimes the neighborhood (when my father chose to take his anger out into the street) into an alienating turmoil. And even though I live every day with flashes of terror, precipitated by my father's relentless outbursts, I don't blame her for her decision and courses of action. She learned to live with the cards that were dealt her, to adjust to her changing fortunes, as did I.

The lobby of the hotel was crammed with the baggage of those guests taking leave of their sweatbox rooms and dissatisfied customers complaining to helpless hotel personnel; I fled from the confusion and went into the bar. The place was jumping and the atmosphere was rather festive. I ordered a Budweiser. "It's not cold anymore, but it's still got a chill," the bartender told me.

"Whatever," I said.

"This is the greatest night," the bartender said. "Nobody cares about anything, except for sitting down and getting soused. It's like the good old days when people used to hang out in bars."

"You mean the good old days before marijuana?"

"No," he said, "I mean before Perrier."

"I hate Perrier," a woman standing at the bar beside me, said. She was not talking to me or the bartender or anyone else in particular, but more to the world at large—and to herself. I sensed that she didn't care one way or another if anyone paid any attention. "And I hate the whole goddamn water culture and the idea of people drinking water out of little plastic bottles," she continued.

She was an attractive curly-haired brunette, medium build. Her fingernails were colored in a range of frosted pastel shades, and she had a face with a perpetual smile—as if everything she said, thought, observed, and overheard was amusing. "People walk the streets with water bottles in their hands, taking periodic sips," she continued. "This pisses me off. My ex-boyfriend carried a plastic water bottle wherever he went, sipping. Except in his case, he was slurping—big splashy sucking noises—like a dog. When we were out on walks. When we went to movies. He carried a water bottle and slurped. He took night classes at Georgetown University with a fucking water bottle in his book bag. Went to work on a bus with a water bottle. First thing after making love was cracking a fresh Aquaviva. *Slurp. Slurrrrp.* Drove me crazy. I couldn't take it. Got to the point that when I began to think about him, you know, fantasize and stuff? . . ."

This was a question rather than a statement. I nodded and smiled. She had the same eyes as my wife Patricia—round and wild, like balls in roulette wheels, the world whirling around her and she looking for a place to rest in the middle, before the next spin. Random numbers and the balls careening to catch up.

"His penis emerged as a water bottle," she said. "I was giving head to a plastic pop-top."

I nodded again. But I wasn't smiling. Sexual allusions were no longer funny to me. At Patricia's request, we hadn't shared the same room, let alone the same bed, for a long time. Gradually, our sexual moratorium led to additional isolation, as I tried to provide her with the space she needed to examine our failing relationship with distance and clarity, just as I was seeking clarity through distance now.

I traveled as much as I could, giving readings, conducting workshops and seminars across the country, scheduling meetings to raise money for my literary journal, *Creative Nonfiction*. When James Wolcott had branded me a "human octopus" for being so involved in so many different aspects of creative nonfiction and such an outspoken and involved spokesperson for the genre, he did not know or care why I was so driven. Previously, I had practiced the writer's life and creative nonfiction like a religion, writing relentlessly at my regular 4:30 A.M.-to-noon schedule and immersing myself in as many places as possible, meeting new people and having unusual experiences. The demands of *Creative Nonfiction* and the arrival of my son, Sam, had caused a significant shift in my priorities, but I was still writing and teaching. Wolcott and others did not know that I was also reacting to a crisis period in my life—not running away, but simply removing myself to give Patricia the space she desired.

But it wasn't working—not for me or Patricia. I felt like a grade-school kid who had misbehaved and was made to sit in a corner apart from his friends and classmates. But I hadn't misbehaved—that was the irony. It was my wife who had gone haywire, and I was paying for it—in detention and isolation—away from my son, whom I desperately missed.

"Do you want to know what I said when he asked me to marry him?" the woman continued.

"Sure. What did you say?"

"Put your lips where your heart is," I told him. "Marry your fucking water bottle."

She looked at me, smiling and nodding, as if she wanted me to encourage her to continue. "I like seltzer, myself," I said.

"Bubble guys are a gas," she said, suddenly laughing uproariously.

"What are you drinking?" I said. It actually took me about thirty seconds to understand her joke.

"Scotch," she said.

"Another Scotch," I told the bartender,

"Are you trying to pick me up?" the woman said.

"I'm trying to buy you a drink," I said.

I'm not shy with women, but her questions made me feel awkward. Was she flirting with me? Was I flirting with her? Should I tell her that I am married? "*Am* I married?" I asked myself. What are a husband's responsibilities to a wife who has called a sexual moratorium in order to decide whether or not to leave him—a moratorium that has lasted four years?

The woman tilted the glass of ice and Scotch with her multi-painted fingertips and sipped. "Tell me your name is Angelo," she said.

"You want me to tell you my name is Angelo, whether it is Angelo or not?"

"Your name's not Angelo?"

"Only if you want me to be Angelo, then I'll be Angelo."

"I don't want you to be Angelo if you're not really Angelo," she said. "But to tell the truth, I don't want to talk if your name's not Angelo. If your name's not Angelo, you'll have to get away from me. If your name's not Angelo, you're definitely cramping my style because I am waiting for Angelo to see me. Angelo doesn't know me yet, but he's supposed to be looking for me at this very moment."

Angelo was to be her blind date for the evening. They had first connected through the personals section of a local newspaper. Many of her dates came through that venue, and I found out later that the water bottle guy to whom she had been temporarily engaged had also first contacted her via the personals date-link. At the beginning of her telephone conversation with Angelo, she "had no interest," she said. "I was about ready to interrupt whatever he was saying, tell him he was a Philistine and hang up the phone— until he told me his profession."

"Which was?" I asked.

"Angelo is a Marine Corps intelligence officer."

"Guys with clandestine professions turn you on?" I asked.

"No," she said, "not really." She sighed and her voice dropped, got caught in her throat. And for the first time I could see that there was another side to her manic nonstop edge of banter. Even her perpetual smile began to waver. "My father was also a Marine Corps intelligence officer," she told me. "He was killed somewhere in 1964, but I don't know where. The Marine Corps never told my mother anything, except that he was dead or missing in action. We don't know, although we can safely assume that he didn't even have a proper funeral. I was born in 1960. In my whole life, I saw my dad twice and I don't remember anything that happened either time."

"The first time I saw my father, he was also in the military—or just recently discharged," I interrupted. "He hit me because I didn't listen to my grandmother when she told me to stop playing with knickknacks on the coffee table."

"Get a grip," she said. "He was doing what he needed to do, making you into a responsible kid."

"I have heard that before," I said. "There's an entire generation of redneck fascists who follow the 'spare the switch and spoil the child' philosophy."

"I was desperate for some discipline in my life. Living alone with my mother I was a spoiled brat."

"I wouldn't have ever guessed," I said, sipping from my beer. "You seem very well-adjusted."

She glanced at me sharply, but continued talking without pause. "I'd rather have a father who beat the shit out of me than a father who was never there."

"I'd rather have a father who never beat the shit out of me who was almost always there," I replied.

She paused and considered: "I guess that doesn't seem too much to ask."

There were many parallels between this woman and my wife, Patricia, beginning with their father's connection to the military. Patricia's father fought in World War II, as did mine, but came home a different man—distant and somewhat uncommunicative. His heart was overseas, imbued with the frenzy and brotherhood of battle. Life working as a service person for a public utility hardly duplicated the camaraderie and the edgy tension to which he had become addicted. His ambivalence toward family and home life had created a bitterness and anger. He took refuge at the neighborhood tavern. Her mother, left alone, vented her frustration on her daughter.

"There's not a lot good I can say about being strapped on the ass or slapped in the face by your parent." I was referring not only to my own experiences, but also Patricia's.

"I am truly sorry," she said. "I've missed having a man in my life. I mean a father-man, a leader and advisor and a male role model. I guess I am forgetting that there could be a down side."

But I was thinking now of how very much my son was going to miss me as he grew older, if I listened to Patricia and left the house—gave her even more space to decide what she wanted to do and allowed her to determine the fate of our marriage. Which is what she wanted: for me to move out and for Sam to stay with her.

Sam may not know now how important a good father can be since, as a toddler, he is still attached at the hip to his mom. But one of the reasons I wanted to be a father was to make up to Sam what I had been denied as a boy, to prove to myself that I could be a good father, that being a good father was in reach of the ordinary person, like my own father—like any man with love in his heart and with the courage to commit himself to the task, no matter how daunting. That's not only the key to fatherhood; that's the key to every challenge in life: to make a commitment, to honor that commitment, and to never walk away until there are no other options. Besides, a child, boy or girl, deserves a good father; Patricia and I had both had fathers. But neither of them served meritoriously, with honor, which is the only way a father or mother should serve. Nothing less can be expected.

Right at this moment in time, Patricia and I had options to play out, which will affect Sam. I assume my parents had options, although they did not have the fatherly therapist to help them recapture a long-lost friendship. It occurred to me that that period of a few hours, long ago when my mother had fled with me into the park in our family car, was her own attempt to find clarity through escape and distance. I don't know, and I have never asked her what happened that made her decide to return to my father, why she did not drive directly to her parents' house—they lived on the other side of the park—or to Atlantic City, New Jersey, or Brooklyn, New York, or anywhere we could have started a new life, free of his intimidating temper, his irritating nagging for perfection, his dark and brooding silences when things did not go his way. Had something happened that made her come back? Or did she leave knowing from the start that she would inevitably return?

The woman who lost her teeth popped into my mind. To this point, I had not thought of her in relation to my mother's escape in the family car or her reluctance to leave my father, but the image came back to me. There was Mollie Gutkind, sitting in the park, halfway between my home and her parents' house, with a five-year-old child whimpering at her feet, begging her to divorce her husband. Mollie Gutkind, who had been to Clarksburg, West Virginia, Philadelphia, Cleveland, and New York, but never anywhere else—ever.

It wasn't as alienating and frightening as the Chicago bus station might have seemed to a country person who had never been more than thirty miles from the house in which she was born, but to a woman raised during war and depression, sheltered similarly in her own neighborhood by a caring, close-knit family, assuming responsibility for a child, on her own, it must have been equally daunting and bizarre.

"And you thought this Angelo would help you find that male role model?" I asked the water bottle woman.

"I thought Angelo would help me feel something, that's all. I hate not feeling anything toward my father. Even if the feeling isn't good, I want to feel something: hatred, animosity, love, whatever. A feeling for my dad will help me go on with my life. But in this fucking blackout, he's probably home and in bed by now. If he gave up getting here, I wouldn't be surprised. I'll probably never meet him."

"So call me Angelo," I said. "If that will make you feel better, and if you are relatively certain he won't be showing up, then let's just pretend I am Angelo. We could have another drink."

"Okay," she replied.

"Your father's name was Angelo?"

"My father, Arthur, was Italian, like Angelo," she said. "And then when I put his profession—Marine Corps Intelligence—together with his name . . . *Angelo, Arthur*, well then I really wanted to meet this guy. My father left me—he was killed before I ever knew him—and I can't feel anything about him," she said, slumping down on a vacant bar stool. "He went away from me. He wouldn't let me know him. It's so hard to love somebody when you don't know who and what in the hell they are. Give me another fucking scotch," she said.

I ordered her drink—and another beer for myself. And I was suddenly struck by the sadness and emptiness this woman conveyed—

a feeling that I, here in Georgetown on this blackout eerie night, profoundly shared. She was not manic and crazy, but lonely and confused, just like the woman who feared losing her teeth.

She returned from Chicago not because she wanted to, but because she had no other choice and nothing else to do. The alternatives—living in Davenport, Iowa, remaining frozen in the Chicago bus station, traveling sporadically until her money ran out or her husband had to come to get her—were unacceptable. But perhaps, she thought, she could go back to her tarpaper shack as a different person. Now she knew that it wasn't so hard to leave her husband, and if she ever wanted to again she would be better prepared; her goals would be more practical and achievable. The fact that she left home and got to Chicago made her stronger, not weaker; it was a way to demonstrate to her husband and to herself exactly what she could do to disrupt their lives. Had that been my mother's plan?

I said to the woman in the bar: "I understand the parallels are not the same, but I feel as abandoned as you. I'm all alone. I don't know what to do. My wife doesn't want me at home. She doesn't want me to be her husband. All I want is to be a father—I no longer care about being a husband—and I feel as if I am being separated from my son by the one person who tried to stop me from having a son." Suddenly I realized that I was crying.

The day my wife announced our divorce came during the same week and month that, four years earlier, she had called the moratorium on sex. It had happened when we returned from Hershey Park, which is an amusement park in Hershey, Pennsylvania, kind of a lowbrow Disney World for chocolate fanatics.

When I was a kid, I had always heard about the wonderful tour of the Hershey Chocolate Factory in which you could watch the entire chocolate-making process unfold, while eating as many Hershey Kisses (droplets of chocolate covered with aluminum foil)—"silver tops" we called them—as parents or teachers allowed. And one of my favorite writers, John McPhee, had once written an article for the *New Yorker* about a man who had worked for Hershey's his entire life and lived on the corner of Chocolate and Vanilla Streets in Hershey, Pennsylvania.

Right before chocolate was about to be poured into molds, bars, or kisses, this fellow would sample each and every batch and, when determining that the taste and consistency were of acceptable quality, would announce, "That's Hershey's." I once heard McPhee say, while being interviewed on National Public Radio, that he practiced the same kind of instinctive quality control in his writing. He knew when an article or essay was ready to send to his editors, because, instinctively, with one reading (a taste) he could tell it was of Hershey's quality—the best possible product.

Unfortunately, however, years before Sam and I reached Hershey Park, the company canceled the factory tours and had, in its place, created a clunky animated version of the chocolate-making process—a train ride through a make-believe chocolate factory that was about as exciting as eating asparagus. And when I telephoned the factory to see if the "That's Hershey's" man was still alive, the people in the public relations department were aghast at the notion that one old man would be allowed to determine the fate of a multi-million-dollar batch of chocolate. Not that they denied the possibility; they just couldn't deal with it. These days, the entire system is automated and computerized; I imagined a computer sampling the bubbling brown brew, with a tongue suddenly unfurled from somewhere inside the CD compartment.

When we arrived home, Patricia had arranged for my brother to spend the evening with Sam. I was surprised because we had originally intended to have a family dinner. Once we were alone, it didn't take long for her to announce her intention. "I love you like a friend, but not a husband."

It was then that I became aware of the distant blood-curdling shriek of something dying. No words—just this animalistic death song, slow, soulful, agonizing, enveloping my body. I had never heard such a horrifying, bone-chilling sound. It wrapped around my ears, coursed through my blood like a twisting, rabid organism. I began shaking, felt my shoulder slamming repeatedly into the bedroom wall. My wife's eyes were steadfast and unyielding. She too listened to that soulful elongated shriek of desperation, an agony that I will never forget, that I eventually realized was coming from my own lips, emanating from deep inside of me.

"Ain't this blackout wonderful," the woman said. She put her arm around my shoulders. Now she too was crying.

"This blackout could go on forever, as far as I'm concerned," I said.

"It's so safe and secure. The world is in limbo," she said. "We can say anything to one another, it wouldn't matter. We don't know each other's names, and we don't want to know each other's names. But I do wish you were Angelo."

"So do I," I said. "Angelo or somebody else. I sure wish I wasn't myself. I never imagined this would happen to me, I swear to God. I thought when my son was born that we would be a family, the three of us, together for the rest of our lives."

"The world beats you down," the woman said. "Circumstances having nothing to do with you, per se. It is the way of the world— the natural downward direction of life. I was ready for Angelo. I was up for it. Then this blackout fucked me over. It is all my fault."

"You can't blame yourself for the blackout."

"And why not?" she laughed. "Maybe I turned on too many lights this evening. I drained just enough juice to strain the limits and force the entire power plant into overload. Little old me, all by myself. Like my psychiatrist always says, 'You are your own worst enemy.'"

After walking the woman back to her car and kissing her good night, I returned to the Georgetown Inn and negotiated my way up the backstairs to my fifth-floor room. The windows were locked and painted shut. I undressed in the pasty, oppressive heat, remembering the pasty oppressive summer nights in Pittsburgh, when I was a young teenager, and my father would punish me when I was working for him in his shoe store, locking me in the basement. Sometimes if he was really angry, he would douse the lights and I would grope my way to the only seat in the cellar—the toilet seat—and sit there huddled against the commode shivering in the dark.

I woke up in the bathroom the following morning, soaked with sweat, my body draped like a wet blanket over the commode, stiff and hung over, empty and desperate inside, thinking about the woman's final comment that we are our own worst enemies.

I refused to accept what she was saying.

Was I the person who ruined my life? I did not believe that that was true. Did I cause my father to mistreat and hurt me? Did I do something so terrible to my wife that forced her to abandon me and break up our family? On the contrary. I had tried to treat my father with deference and to follow his orders, no matter how arbitrary, to the best of my ability. As to my wife, I always serviced her account, so to speak, gave her what she wanted: a house I did not like in a neighborhood I didn't want to live in; space, time, freedom to return to school or the working world. The fact that she could not make up her mind about how she wanted to use her freedom and was therefore home with me everyday in the house where I worked, "under siege," as she had once said, was not my fault. My presence made her feel "pressed in." But I had worked at home long before I knew her.

The irony was that I was the person who had pushed for a family—not my wife, who hated families, hers especially, and had done everything possible to stonewall our connections with other people, family and friends included. Now, at this very moment, I lay on a bathroom floor in a hot, stinking, unventilated, unlit hotel room, while my wife was cuddling comfortably with the child I had fought and begged for—for a decade. In fact, she was in New Jersey with my oldest friends, to whom I had introduced her. Now they were her friends, too, and I was in isolation from everyone I loved.

Maybe the woman from the hotel bar was right. We can cause a great deal of our own unhappiness because we feel guilty and intimidated by other people. My father said that I was not a good son, and I believed him because, after all, he was my father. And I believed my wife, who blamed me for her unhappiness, and I punished myself by separating myself from the child I had wanted so desperately for so long. What had she said to me once on a beach near Santa Barbara, California, during a vacation marred by bickering about children? "I will never be a mother. I will never have a child. You will never convince me. I refuse to talk about it. I don't want to live life with the responsibility of anybody else." I realized the irony and twist in the scenario. She was now living the life I had wanted, while I was relegated to the isolation for which she had so heatedly battled.

It was at that moment that I stopped being my own worst enemy. I packed my bags, canceled my meetings, and joined my family and friends in New Jersey. Anytime my wife wanted to leave me, she could, I decided—and eventually she did. But I would be home with my son, whenever possible and for as long as possible. My decision was irrevocable. It set me free.

Waiting Away

I was in the office of a dermatologist who, while tearing into the plantar's wart on my right foot, glanced curiously up at my chest. "Wait," she murmured, "Melanoma."

At the time, I did not know precisely what melanoma was, but I knew the word to which it was most associated: cancer. She tenderly touched the mole she had spotted as the likely suspect and commented: "I don't think this is malignant, but you need to have it removed immediately." She paused and continued in a hushed voice. "Not that I want to worry you." I braced myself for what was coming next. "But, three weeks from now, in a worst-case scenario, you could be dead."

I smiled bravely. "I thought you didn't want to worry me."

She did not smile back. "You need to see a surgeon."

"Well I don't know a surgeon," I said. "Who's the best in Pittsburgh?"

She replied immediately with a name that, for purposes of this essay, I have changed: "Sidney Schwartz."

"Can you make the arrangements?"

"I'll take care of everything, Mr. Gutkind."

I did not like the way she suddenly called me by my last name. Through all of our associations related to my plantar's wart, we had been on a first-name basis. Now that I was three weeks away from a painful demise, she had immediately adopted what I have come to call the "doctor's distance declaration," which establishes a direct line of withdrawal from patient interaction in proportion to severity of illness and prognosis for recovery. The more serious and potentially fatal the malady, the more physicians will study your chart and contemplate their geeky shoes, tending to walk backwards whenever the patient or family members attempt to ask question or talk with them.

Sidney Schwartz was my prototype of this syndrome. First, his nurse said that he did not need to meet me. Such a minor procedure required no personal contact or preliminary assessment. Second, it would be ten days before I could be squeezed into his schedule. And this, of course, was a favor performed on behalf of the referring dermatologist, a long-time colleague. Otherwise, it would have been a month. I appreciated the consideration. However, having done a little research about melanoma and learning how quickly it might spread, the ten days waiting with the dark specter of death I now perceived hanging over my head was one of the most anxious periods of my life. Those ten days were nothing compared to the sheer terror of the day of the surgery.

I arrived at the Outpatient Surgical Center (OPSC) at 7 A.M. for my pre-op examination. I was weighed. My pulse was taken. The necessary forms were filled out, my clothes and personal items stored away safely in a locker at the other end of the unit. I put on one of those paper hospital robes, a miniskirt model that hung about three inches above my knees, along with paper hospital booties. A nurse led me to a tiny windowless room, invited me to make myself comfortable. Dr. Schwartz was due at 8 A.M. and we were a little early.

I was immediately bored and jumpy as I waited. I had been so focused on the impending surgery that I hadn't even thought to bring anything to read. But I knew that Dr. Schwartz, the best surgeon in Pittsburgh, would be arriving any minute to interrupt whatever reading or work I might be doing, anyway. Even at 9 A.M., when there was no sign of Dr. Schwartz or any other doctor who might be coming to check in with me, I was confident that it was only a matter of a little more time. It would have been naive of me to assume that surgeons would be any more punctual about surgery than other physicians were in keeping appointments. Besides, there were sick people throughout the city needing emergency surgery, bleeding to death on an operating table. A heroic Sidney Schwartz was obviously laboring to save one of them. In the back of his mind, Schwartz knew that I was waiting at the OPSC—and he would be rushing in here any second, breathless, spouting apologies while sharpening his scalpel, getting down to business.

I continued to believe that until around 11 A.M. when one of the nurses came in to say that she had initially been told that Sidney Schwartz had been sidetracked by an emergency procedure, but was no longer certain that that was true. He wasn't answering his page and no one, including his partners, could find him. She was more embarrassed than apologetic—and she was whispering, as if confiding a dark secret or committing a crime, which, in this doctor-friendly milieu, she was. Around lunchtime, the nurse reported that someone had seen Sidney Schwartz in the hospital in surgical scrubs and heading this way, but when he did not show up by 1 P.M. she contacted the operator who began to page him over the hospital intercom. There were fourteen separate pages over the next hour and a half—I counted every one of them as I sat, a prisoner in that windowless waiting room, listening to the hum of the air conditioner and the muffled activity in the hallway behind my closed door. The hollow persistent sound of the paging operator summoning Schwartz to the Outpatient Surgical Center triggered within me a new and more acute wave of anxiety and fear. Periodically, I wandered out of my room and inquired at the nurse's station for an update. Twice I used the nurse's phone to call Schwartz's office to complain, but after being frozen in "hold" limbo for many minutes as Schwartz's secretaries were attempting to locate him, I hung up the phone and retreated back to my cell.

At 3 P.M., when the nurse came in carrying my clothes to apologetically announce that her shift was over and that the entire unit was closing down for the day, I was a complete wreck. To me, this was an omen, a clear message that the melanoma was malignant and that I was going to die. After all, the dermatologist had provided her worst-case scenario—"three weeks"; nearly half of the last days of my life had already been wasted waiting for Sidney Schwartz, the best surgeon in Pittsburgh, to stand me up. This was torture: eight hours in a windowless waiting room, no television, radio, or reading material. Even convicted murderers were given breakfast, lunch, perhaps a walk in the "yard" for fresh air—and real clothes. You could hardly take a walk in the yard in a paper miniskirt and pastel blue booties.

In retrospect, it was a mistake to have arrived at the OPSC without a friend to keep me company or demand help, but I was recently divorced and feeling as if I needed to confront the challenges of life on my own without leaning on a partner. Later, collapsing at home in my bed, I listened to the messages on my answering machine. The last one was from a secretary in Schwartz's office explaining that in the frenetic rush of his day, Dr. Schwartz had simply overlooked my procedure and that he would be pleased to reschedule for the following week. She offered a couple of dates and times and suggested that I return her call if I was interested. I wasn't.

I wrote a number of letters, never sent, and composed a slew of speeches, never delivered, to Dr. Schwartz over a long period of years. Not that I was afraid of Sidney Schwartz or too sick from chemotherapy (which, in fact, never happened—I found another surgeon who removed the mole a few days later, which, after a quick biopsy, was judged benign). The truth is, I never confronted Dr. Schwartz. I was too enraged to simply yell and scream and bash his head in; rather, I wanted to humiliate Sidney Schwartz in front of his colleagues, friends, and family—the people who most respected him. My dream was that I would serendipitously come into contact with him one day, face to face, preferably at a dinner party. He wouldn't know me, but I would know him, and I would charm and befriend him, along with everyone else at the table, all the while gently guiding the conversation toward the issues of ethics and morality in medicine—the Hippocratic Oath, the physician's responsibility to the patient, all the good stuff about which physicians love to expound, at which point I would begin my melanoma story in basically the same way I have started the story here, by describing the dermatologist, and the hour-by-hour, soul-twisting torture in the windowless room waiting for the surgeon to appear. But I wouldn't say the surgeon's name—not for a while.

I'd wait for the precise moment, skillfully unfolding the details of the story and building suspense and curiosity about the identity of the surgeon, dropping a few subtle, pointed clues. In this scenario, I can literally picture all of the people at the long dinner table, spellbound, heads strained forward to listen as the scenes and incidents I relate gallop toward the conclusion. And I can also picture the object of my anger, Sidney Schwartz, growing ever more uncomfortable in his chair as the intimate nature of my story finally begins to touch some inner chord of awareness. I know in my heart that he is beginning to suspect the humiliating reality approaching him. At the end of the story, with my companions primed and totally empathetic and with my final words of dismay echoing through the quiet, darkening dining room, someone breaks the silence and asks: "Who was this horrible doctor?"

At which point, I carefully place the coffee cup in its saucer and turn ever so slowly toward my nemesis, my enemy, the object of my pent-up, bone-scraping rage, Sidney Schwartz, and look him straight in the eye, as I quietly announce: "He is sitting among us at this table."

It was this dream of revenge, through the consummate humiliation of Sidney Schwartz specifically and my melanoma experience generally, that led me eventually to write about medicine and science. What kind of people could devise a system in a world with the Hippocratic Oath as the bedrock of healing, that would engender such an impersonal and unresponsive atmosphere, I wondered? Why is a medical center designed to function primarily for its doctors, rather than for the patients it is supposedly created to treat and serve? Here, of course, I was thinking of Sidney Schwartz, who stood me up in the operating room and never felt the need to apologize for his actions, and of the hospital, which allowed surgeons to behave boorishly, as long as they saved lives. Not that lifesaving is bad—or shouldn't be a preeminent surgical responsibility and goal. But patients needn't be traumatized in the process through physician insensitivity.

On the organ transplant service, which is where I anchored my first medically oriented book, I listened to a prominent surgeon impatiently interrupt a resident, who was explaining a procedure to a family member, prompting him to "save lives first—answer questions later." Another surgeon told me, in defense of his insensitive behavior, "Psychological trauma and all that stuff is important, but it doesn't make a goddamn difference if you are well-adjusted and dead."

The thing was, I had gotten to know the men responsible for these insensitive comments during the process of my research, and I was fond of them both. I knew that what they meant at the moment the remarks were made was that they had no time to act nice; now it was time to act immediately. Every second counted if their patient was to live. It was unfortunate if the patient or the patient's family and friends didn't like their surgeons, but surgeons weren't selected because of their personality. "I don't care whether you like me or not," a pediatric surgeon once told a patient, as I listened. "My only real job is to give your home a healthy child, and if I can do that, you're going to love me, even though you might also hate my guts." Indeed, I had never met or interviewed Sidney Schwartz; he was chosen because I was told he was the best person for the job. Which doesn't mean he should be forgiven for standing me up or that surgeons be permitted boorish or egocentric behavior, which is often part of the surgical personality.

Sidney Schwartz almost died—many years after the day he stood me up on the operating table, of hepatitis, contracted, I am told, from one of his patients. When I heard about Sidney Schwartz's disease, I have to admit to a momentary tinge of elation—not because I wanted him to die or to be in pain but in the sudden and pleasing awareness that there was some sort of prevailing justice on this earth. If his colleagues began to pull away from him, he too would have the experience of being the unempowered patient rather than the all-powerful doctor. I doubt that the justice I imagined actually came about in Sidney Schwartz's case, but I am vengeful enough to hope that it did, especially now that I know, in retrospect, that Schwartz received a liver transplant (ironically, had it been a few years earlier I might have observed or scrubbed-in on the procedure). He survived and returned to his practice, a result that is not nearly as routine as the medical community or the media might lead an unaware consumer to believe. In fact, I am told that he recently built a new and luxurious house in my neighborhood, although I still don't know what he looks like and I have no interest in finding out.

Charlie Looks Good

We were going to Hackensack, New Jersey, for a cousin's bar mitzvah and would be coming back home in thirty-six hours. This was the first trip I had taken with my parents since I was a kid, when we would pile into the car to drive to Wildwood, New Jersey, two hundred miles south, where we rented an apartment next door to my Uncle Morris (the family real-estate mogul, who owned his own beach house). It occurred to me as we staggered with our luggage into the terminal at the Greater Pittsburgh International Airport this particular morning that I hardly ever saw my parents outside their home anymore. It was more convenient if I and my son Sam and my brother Richard visited their house—the one in which Richard and I grew up—where our roles were clearly defined.

My father, an egg-shaped, balding man of eighty-three, was struggling with a corrugated cardboard box he had been lugging from the car into the terminal. Without asking, Richard decided to help. He snatched the box from my father's hand and flung it up over his shoulder—and then he almost toppled over backwards. "What's in this?" he asked. My father didn't answer.

"If your father wants to bring a package on an airplane, then what's stopping him?" my mother said.

"I'm not trying to stop him," Richard said. "But it's heavy."

"So?" my mother said.

"So do *you* want to carry it?" Richard asked. He was also carrying my parents' suitcase.

My mother held up her purse, newspaper, and a plastic bag containing a couple of out-of-date women's magazines and shrugged. "I'm loaded down."

At the security checkpoint, the box warranted closer examination. A guard untied and unpacked it, revealing a half-dozen oversized glass canisters of dried fruit and concentrated soup mixes, a gift for my other brother, Michael, Richard's twin, and his wife, who would be meeting us. There were two milk cartons filled with two thousand pennies each, collected over the year for grandson Jonathan. Nice enough gifts, but heavy, more appropriate for shipping UPS. After the inspection, my father hurriedly repacked and retied his cardboard box, a little less neatly than before. As we headed down the ramp toward our gate, the twine my father had used to pack the box began unraveling. We stopped to retie it once, then again. But soon the twine was cutting into Richard's hand, blocking circulation. And the weight was hurting his chronically misaligned back. About halfway to the gate, my mother had to go to the bathroom. And then my father had to go to the bathroom. And then Richard had to go to the bathroom. Meanwhile, Sam was upset with my mother's shoes.

Sam read everything—menus, billboards. Bedtime reading included manuals to electronic appliances or computer software, a habit reflected in his advanced vocabulary. Last time in an airplane, Sam carefully examined the laminated card tucked in the seat pouch, outlining the exits and evacuation procedures and explaining the dos and don'ts of in-flight travel, which included unauthorized footwear for emergency exits. Which is why he began pointing down at my mother's medium-heel black-leather pumps. "Bubbie's shoes are high heels and therefore disallowed," Sam announced.

"What's he saying? My shoes are illegal?" my mother asked. She's a short woman, torpedo chested, neatly preserved, but increasingly timid, wary of the growing complexities of the outside world. Now she insisted that she stop and change. She knew exactly where her flat shoes were located, although when she looked inside her suitcase, she remembered that she had forgotten them. She repacked her bag, while I closed my eyes and turned my back, pretending that this was not happening and that I had no connection with the woman rummaging through her suitcase in the middle of the terminal and the man (my father), a fashion plate in the red-plaid double-knit trousers, with white belt and matching white shoes.

We heard the announcement for our flight starting to board. "There goes our brilliant time-saving plan about getting on board first," Richard said. Assuming that U.S. Airways Saturday morning from Pittsburgh to Newark would be a full flight, we had intended to arrive early and board as soon as possible to assure space in the overhead compartment for our carry-on luggage. This would have allowed us to deplane quickly, pick up our rental car, and get to Hackensack before the bar mitzvah started.

I shrugged. "At least we're going to make it."

And we did make it—on time—to the gate, that is. But when the ticket agent asked for a picture ID, my father answered: "I don't have my wallet."

"Neither do I," my mother said.

"You don't have your driver's licenses?" the ticket agent said.

My father shook his head. "I thought we were flying."

"No identification?" Richard repeated.

"I have birth marks," my father said. I looked at him carefully. Was he joking? "Don't you think you ought to carry some official identification when you go out of town?" I asked.

"What for?" my mother said. "Don't you know who I am? You'll tell anyone who asks."

"But what happens if you drop dead? I might not be around to identify you."

"Who cares who's there to identify me if I'm dead?" my father said.

"What are we going to do?" my mother said.

"Do?" I repeated. Suddenly, angrily, I turned to my mother: "What is wrong with you, not bringing identification? How could you be so . . ."

Before I could finish my sentence—or even figure out what else I wanted to say—my mother whirled around and began to wag her finger in the same way she had wagged that finger, repeatedly, threateningly, many years ago.

"Look, Lee, you may be considered a big shot in some places, but to me you're just a kid—*my* kid. The person who raised you was me. And I've been around. I didn't come to this country yesterday, you know." Then she paused and lowered her voice. She had been shouting, I suddenly realized; people were staring. A man I knew from the university where I teach was walking by. We nodded into the embarrassing silence.

The conversation between my family and the ticket agent continued. I walked away and let Richard handle it. I was disgusted and embarrassed both because they were my parents and also because, as my parents, they represented what and whom I could one day become. I wasn't afraid of getting old, at least literally, not as much as I feared *acting* old, losing touch with the world and my children, as my parents have lost touch with us and everything else around them, except the inside of their house and their closest remaining friends, a dwindling slow-moving bunch. And I also feared losing my parents, for despite my resentments, the fact I have never been able to avoid is that I still need them. The longer they are alive, the less vulnerable and more secure I feel, especially now that I, a divorced single father, have Sam to support and protect.

Eventually an airline supervisor decided that my mother and father posed no significant threat to the flight. Then my father went to the bathroom. After about ten minutes, we started to wonder what had happened to him. Now the flight was pretty much boarded. The ticket agents were looking at their watches and glancing at us anxiously. "I'll go and see what's keeping Jack," Richard said, hurrying down the corridor toward the "Restrooms" sign. We had always referred to our parents by first names when discussing them, Jack and Mollie.

Meanwhile, I apologized to my mother. I told her that I had no business showing such disdain. As a child, I had wanted my mother to eliminate my father from our lives, but to her, keeping the family together was of paramount importance. Ironically, this was the same rationale I had used with my wife—unsuccessfully—when my wife had first broached the subject of divorce—keeping the family intact for the sake of Sam.

We had about two minutes before the gate was to be shut and we would lose our seats when Richard came running down the corridor from the restroom. He was flushed, breathless and laughing. My mother and I and Sam went to meet him. "What happened to Jack?" I said.

"That's what I wanted to find out when I walked into the bathroom," Richard said.

"Is he sick?" my mother interrupted.

"But no one seemed to be there," Richard continued. "I called his name, but nobody answered."

"No one was in the bathroom?" I said.

"No one was answering. I thought Jack was dead or something— from carrying that box. So I got down on my hands and knees and looked under the stall doors for his feet."

"So what did you see?" I asked.

"I saw . . . high heels."

"Your father was wearing high heels?" my mother asked.

"High heels are prohibited on airplanes," Sam said.

Richard ignored them both. "Then someone came into the bathroom, walked up behind me, and tapped me on the shoulder. I jumped up, turned around."

"Was it Jack?" I asked.

"No," Richard said.

"Who was it then?"

"A woman!"

"Don't tell me," I said. "You were . . ."

"That's right," Richard interrupted. "I was in the lady's room."

"Oh my God!" said my mother.

"I was so embarrassed, I started running out of the place—backwards," Richard said. "I almost killed another lady I crashed into when I was backing out. Then the security guard saw me. 'What do you think you are doing?' he said."

" 'I was looking for my father.' "

" 'In the *lady's* room?' "

"I can't believe you went to the lady's room," my mother said.

"It was an innocent mistake," said Richard.

We were standing at the gate ready to board, the four of us

slightly nervous about my father's whereabouts, but laughing with Richard at his funny story, when my father finally appeared. He was carrying the cardboard box, which he had taken into the men's room with him. But it had been a long morning, and he was very tired now, leaning over to one side and limping in slow motion down the corridor like a sinking ship.

I touched him on the shoulder and when he turned, I reached out towards him. He handed over the box without comment.

I dropped my parents and Richard at the synagogue entrance and began cruising the streets, eventually squeezing our rental Ford between a battered station wagon with a "Sabbath at the Seaside" bumper sticker and a gleaming silver Mercedes Benz 300SL. After we parked, Sam decided to run, but in no more than ten steps he tripped, fell on the sidewalk, and started to scream. I lifted him up (his legs always turn to noodles when he is hurt or angry) and carried him on my shoulders. There was a brief moment of silence as we neared the steps to the rather drab fifties' style building, then a blood-curdling shriek. "What's wrong?" I said, lowering him to the ground. "What is it?"

Sam was staring down at a droplet of blood on his finger. "I need a Band-Aid," he sobbed. I had forgotten a handkerchief, so I blotted the blood with the only available cloth—the back of my silk tie, a gesture that I knew would only temporarily sooth him. I discovered the janitor in an alleyway at the rear entrance, smoking a cigarette and moving around some trash bags. Years ago, the only non-Jew permitted in an Orthodox synagogue was "the Sabbath goy," the non-Jewish person hired to unlock and lock the synagogue (shul), answer phones, and basically perform required maintenance chores. Orthodoxy prohibits work on the Sabbath for the Jewish people, but not gentiles. The janitor led us to a serviceable first-aid kit in the kitchen in an ancient metal box bolted to the wall. Sam balked when I revealed the ordinary Johnson & Johnson Plastic Strips ("I want 3M Brights," meaning the Technicolor kind with the medicated pads), but soon sensed he had pushed me to my limits Band-Aid-wise and backed off.

"Where is everybody?" I asked after I finished "treating" Sam's finger.

The janitor pointed to the ceiling. The chapel is too small to accommodate the Saturday crowd for events with many out-of-town guests, so proceedings are often moved to the recreation hall on the second floor, where folding chairs are set up. The good weather this day in the early spring had precipitated an even larger turnout, which had caused a delay, and which was why the service was still going on. There were nearly three hundred people crammed into this spare area, almost all of whom I did not know. As we entered, I saw Richard and my mother and dad, who had found seats together, and I eventually picked out my other brother Michael and his family, who had driven here this morning from Philadelphia.

My first sight of Cousin Larry, the father of Lane, the bar mitzvah boy, astonished me. My mother, who keeps in touch with our relatives, had observed that Larry had succumbed to the Gutkind family curse—gluttony. Seeing him in the flesh (an understatement), after twenty-five years, I confess to a shameful, buoyant feeling of triumph. After all, I was the cousin who had graduated high school weighing 220 in a size forty-four "husky" suit—not Larry, now sitting like a bloated Buddha with his thick legs crossed and his forearms wrapped around his waist as if he were holding in his stomach. Ironically, when Larry first came to Pittsburgh from Queens, New York, he was the heartthrob of the high school, a John Travolta look-alike who could walk the wise-guy walk and talk the wise-guy talk like few kids in our tight little neighborhood, Squirrel Hill. Considering his "look" and the potential of his New York charisma, Larry could have been exceedingly popular if he hadn't been so focused on how cool he was and how much more he knew about life than anyone else.

Larry had not come to Pittsburgh willingly; his father had died and his mother, my Aunt Ethel, knew that her son's hot-shot, wise-guy persona should be toned down and that my father, Larry's uncle, would be a male presence and role model, as would Uncle Lew, sister Hattie's husband.

But from the beginning, Jack, Ethel, Hattie, Lew (until he died in the middle 1970s) and my mother Mollie bickered over inconsequential matters, such as which of us—Larry or me—was the better and the most promising of the two kids. There was no doubt about who was better looking. Larry won hands down. And neither Larry nor I were superior intellects; we both graduated high school in the lower fifth of our classes. Over the succeeding years, I gradually began to find myself professionally as a writer, while Larry never seemed to be able to get started or sustain any project he managed to begin. After high school, he was in and out of colleges and auto mechanics trade schools for more than a decade. He's been a dispatcher for a small bus company for sixteen years. But the family appreciated Larry's very considerable personal accomplishments: a friendly wife from an upstanding Jewish family from the heart of Hackensack and an intelligent, handsome son, Lane, just as muscular and charismatic as his father had been when young.

My single, lingering memory of my friendship with Larry also took place in a synagogue during the high holidays. In the middle of the service, a man suddenly stood up and waved to another man across the room, announcing quite loudly and to no one in particular, in reference to the person at whom he had just waved, "Charlie looks good!"

Everyone in the synagogue stopped what he or she was doing, including the rabbi and the bar mitzvah boy, and turned to stare first at the man who had spotted and loudly praised Charlie, and then at the man we thought was Charlie. It was difficult to assess how good Charlie actually looked because I had never seen Charlie before and didn't know if there was a time when he looked better or worse. Charlie, obviously embarrassed, was deeply engaged in praying, wrapping his prayer shawl around his head like an old lady's babushka, rocking back and forth and chanting, oblivious to everything going on around him.

"Who the hell is Charlie?" my father had whispered across the aisle to my mother, my aunts, and Uncle Lew. "Is he somebody important?" Nobody knew.

From that point on, Larry and I shared a secret code. When one of our parents or teachers would do something inane or stupid, or when adults, generally, would act immature or foolish, we would turn and look around, pretending we saw someone we knew. Then we would feign excitement, waving and smiling, and exclaim: "It's Charlie! Charlie looks good!" I have never been able to forget this incident; it comes back anytime I meet someone named Charlie— or Charles—or even Chuck. Or when I see an adult do something stupid, I mutter out loud—or think to myself: "Charlie looks good." I have always assumed that Larry experiences a similar "Charlie looks good" déjà vu whenever he witnesses an idiot at work.

For a while, we stood quietly in the back of the room, behind what seemed to be more than three hundred perspiring people, Sam on my shoulders, staring with infatuated relief at the Band-Aid on his finger. "Dad," he said, leaning down and whispering into my ear, while pointing toward the room divider, where the caterers had begun to unveil the traditional Sabbath brunch fish trays, "I'm hungry."

"So am I, Son," I replied, "but services must end and the rabbi must say a prayer—give a blessing—before we can eat."

"But I want a bagel," Sam said, pointing to a table with a basket of bagels that was nearly within our grasp.

"Sam," I said wearily, "give me a break." I was hot, my shoulders were aching, and I was also hungry.

"But Dad," Sam persisted, pointing to the tables and the trays of food. "Look at the people eating . . ." Indeed some of the congregates were getting up, ostensibly to go to the restroom, then ducking down behind the room dividers, snatching bagels, pastries, and other delicacies to devour in privacy behind a locked bathroom door.

Most had been sitting in the synagogue for nearly four hours, while the rabbi and the other men chanted and prayed and bowed through their traditional torah-reading routine, interspersed by periodic contributions from the bar mitzvah boy and the many members of his family. When the service finally ended, the entire congregation, in a blur, stood up, and the room dividers were quickly dragged away. Then the rabbi, a handsome paunchy man with curly graying hair and matching beard, stepped up to the table to recite the blessing. He stood in the middle of that recreation hall, gripping a hunk of challah bread in one hand and a cup of wine in the other, waiting in somber silence for the congregation to come to attention.

The rabbi's lips moved. The prayer was short and sweet: *Baruch uta adenoi eluhenu melach ha-olum, boreye pree hugafen* (Blessed art thou our Lord, King of the Universe) . . . But before he could complete his benediction and wish everyone a happy Sabbath (*Gut Yontif!*) . . . the congregants lost their resolve—and the riot erupted. Three hundred famished men, women, and children, glistening with perspiration and tortured by the seductive aromas of pickled herring in sour-cream sauce, gefilte fish, homemade horse radish, smoked salmon, kosher dills, and pickled beets, simultaneously advanced in a solid mass toward the food tables. Gasping his final words of prayer, the rabbi was pushed aside by the oncoming horde. The last time I saw him, he was backing into the kitchen, clutching a bottle of wine.

Even though we were the tallest humans in the room, with Sam perched on my shoulders, we too were brushed aside by the crowd. Immediately, I signaled Richard and my parents that I would meet them outside. I could mingle with all these New York/New Jersey relatives at the sit-down dinner. Right now, these people were too hungry to be friendly. Cousins I had never met were tossing bagels with cream cheese, sticky cherry Danish, mushy gefilte fish balls, and dill pickle spears to their friends.

Working my way through the churning elbows, the outstretched arms, and the flying food, I flashed on the Philip Roth wedding reception scene in his book *Goodbye Columbus*, in which, during dinner, Marty Krieger, the Kosher Hot Dog King, "a man with as many stomachs as he had chins, and as many heart attacks as chins and stomachs combined," put his hand on his wife's pancake breasts and yelled, "Hey, how about a picture of this?" Meanwhile Tank Feldman devoured baskets of rolls and plates of celery and olives at a record rate, cheered on by his wife Gloria, "who continually looked down the front of her gown as if there was some sort of construction project going on under her clothes." I realized that my extended family had as much class (and gold chains) as the one portrayed by Roth more than thirty years ago.

As I waded through the jostling crowd, I spotted a heavyset man with a red-and-blue-striped tie, who had used a wad of tissue to blot his face of perspiration. Little bits and pieces of white tissue were clinging to his nose, eyebrows, and mustache; a bushy patch of hair growing from his ears had also attracted bits and pieces of tissue, resembling large flecks of dandruff. He was scooping gigantic dollops of egg salad from a fish-shaped mold with a wedge of bread and shoving them into his churning mouth, all the while holding his controlling position at the table by waving a large serving spoon and yelling, "One more bite! One more bite!" Those who ignored his pleas and ventured too close were sprayed with egg salad from the spoon and, if they dared to edge closer, also from his mouth. The man looked familiar.

In addition to my own gluttonous affair, I have hated almost every bar mitzvah reception I have ever attended. The Lane event was no exception. Not many years ago, a bar mitzvah guest knew what to expect: cocktails and hors d'oeuvres, followed by a few sentimental or humorous toasts to the bar mitzvah boy and family, followed by a sit-down dinner. Usually there was a band and dancing, perhaps a separate table for kids. Extravagances were strictly food-oriented: a chopped-liver sculpture of Elvis Presley or a red-caviar dip depicting Moses parting the Red Sea.

These days, guests are tortured and intimidated by a teenage disc jockey whose karaoke microphone is wired into a half-dozen booming, vibrating speakers. In between the loud music, the disc jockey struts around the hall making announcements, interviewing guests on videotape, dancing, singing, and obliterating all possibility for normal human interaction, which is why most people want to come to the bar mitzvah in the first place. What's worse, the disc jockey, working with the family, has choreographed a conglomeration of activities and events designed to make people look as infantile as possible—or bore them to death—in between each course of the dinner.

At this affair, blue-haired bubbies were bunny-hopping before the Jell-O-mold appetizer was served and swinging on the shoulders of their wheezing husbands in a coronary-defying hora after the chicken gumbo soup was slurped down. Lane, Larry, and his wife, Eva, made long presentations to visiting relatives; Lane's best friends gave rambling tributes to Lane and his parents, with stories about Lane's dog, Lane's toys, and even one story about Lane's neighbor's car. Music exploded into the room for dancing in between each presentation, and in between each musical explosion, four high school girls with bare bellies and sequined halters performed, dancing between the tables. The lead girl carried a tambourine, which she slapped vigorously into my ear each time I was engaged in conversation with someone—an annoyance that I eventually came to rely on to keep me awake. The challenge of the evening was to keep my eyes open and my head off the table.

By midnight, when the filet mignon main course was mercifully served, Sam had been asleep, off and on, for two hours—once on the dance floor (on my shoulders), once under the table, and once with his face pillowed on a plate of chicken tenders. Periodically, we went into the bathroom to douse our faces with water; two or three times, I took a jog (with Sam on my shoulders) around the block.

"Dad, why can't we go back to the motel?" Sam pleaded.

"Sam," I told him. "In the Jewish religion, the ceremony in the morning is the supreme test for the bar mitzvah boy, right?" I had previously briefed him on the rules and regulations of bar mitzvahs.

"As to whether he is a man?" Sam asked.

"As to whether he—in this case Lane—can read from the Torah, address the congregation in a mature manner, and demonstrate that he understands he is about to become an adult; he's entering a transition from boy to man. Can you see that?"

Sam nodded. "But the bar mitzvah reception is actually another test—a family loyalty test," I continued. "If you don't suffer through the evening and act like you are having a good time, then you are not considered a good cousin. You could be banned from the family."

Sam looked at me quizzically. "Are you joking?"

"Yes," I replied. "Sort of."

"You won't be banned from the family, but these events symbolize a coming together of your clan—all the people to whom you are related—celebrating the fact that you have raised a child who will soon become an adult and begin to raise his own family."

At the end of the evening, as I was shaking hands goodbye with Larry, the man with the tissue-speckled face who had been holding forth at the egg salad mold at the Saturday reception, walked by. He face was now clean and he seemed normal, as he and Larry nodded, smiled, and waved. "Who is that?" I asked.

"His name is Charlie."

"Are you serious?" I asked, smiling at Larry. "What an amazing coincidence." It was then that I realized my time had come—finally. I had been waiting for years to utter this phrase to someone—the only one—who would understand exactly what it symbolized. I took a deep breath and the words came out. "Charlie looks good!" I said.

I looked at Larry, and he looked at me—and we both nodded and chuckled in mutual appreciation of our shared memory. For the first time since our paths had gone in such conflicting directions, maybe thirty-five years ago, Larry and I had made an intimate connection. It was a magic moment, a frozen second when two people, no matter how different, and despite how history or old wounds or simple misunderstandings have divided them, come together.

I had experienced this connection with my mother the previous day at the airport when I apologized to her and we acknowledged the mutual agony of living with my father, with whom I had also connected when I took the corrugated box from him and our eyes met ever so briefly. It wasn't much, this instantaneous connection, but it represented a mutual point of acceptance and forgiveness.

Perhaps this is why I went to the Lane event in Hackensack—to find out whether there was anything left of my past life that I wanted to keep with me as I ventured further and further from my roots. What I rediscovered was Charlie—who was a metaphor for all of the effort my family invested in competing with one another. In the end, Charlie got his egg salad, just as my parents and Aunt Ethel and Aunt Hattie got a certain amount of satisfaction from their struggles for family dominance. But Ethel and Hattie were both dead—they had missed the highlighting event of Larry's life. And my parents were old and confused; the world had passed them by.

In the end, all of the familial infighting meant nothing. It angered the parents, separated the children, and made the grandchildren strangers. I don't expect to see Larry at any other event, ever, except for my parents' funerals. In a year, Sam and Lane won't recognize each other even if they are sitting side by side in an airplane. The connections that my grandparents nurtured when they came over to America through Ellis Island have run out. The Gutkind family as it was is gone. Now Sam and Lane will take us in different directions.

Desperately Seeking Irene

I was having coffee in a downtown Pittsburgh cafe when I saw through the window Mr. Meyers climbing out of a taxi. Clutching a small overnight bag, he walked quickly up the street. I jumped up and ran outside.

Even from a distance, he looked relatively the same, although a bit chunkier and more pot-bellied. His hair was dark, long over the ears, and as oily as ever. I began to yell. "Mr. Meyers! Mr. Meyers!" He turned, wondering who would call his name in a place where he no longer lived and hadn't visited for years, or at least that's what I imagined he was thinking. Perhaps he didn't see me—or didn't want to see me—or he considered his name to be "Dr. Meyers," not Mr. Meyers, as I had known him before his Ph.D., because I thought he looked right at me before turning his back and hurrying a little faster up the sidewalk.

I appeared to be respectable that day. I was wearing a suit, vest, and striped tie. But seeing Mr. Meyers so suddenly and after so long, made me act a little weird. I began jumping up and down. "Mr. Meyers! Mr. Meyers!" I yelled a little louder when he did not answer. Once again, he turned—and saw me. I should have realized at that point that there would be no reason for Bob Meyers to remember me; he had taught thousands of students over the course of his career. And seeing me jumping and waving crazily and calling his name as it once was—"Mr. Meyers! Mr. Meyers!"—evidently scared him to death because, suddenly, he began to run.

Undaunted, I chased after him, yelling even louder, "Mr. Meyers! Mr. Meyers! Wait! Wait! You don't understand."

But he didn't want to understand. Because when I finally caught up with him blocks later, he was wary and resistant to conversation. I desperately wanted him to know that I was a published author and that I had a tenure-track position teaching creative writing— and that my success was all because of his spontaneous observation and direction in our classroom years ago. I wanted him to feel and understand my gratitude. But in my enthusiasm I had obviously come on too strong—and I couldn't seem to stop myself from pushing and gushing.

I put my hands on his shoulders so I could look him in the eye and he could more clearly see my face. I tried to tell him about my books, about traveling cross-country on a motorcycle and about baseball umpires and the students I was trying to inspire in the way in which he had inspired me. Eventually and reluctantly he listened, quietly and politely, acknowledging that he was happy for my success and pleased that he had been helpful. He even clapped me on the back. Then he was gone, retreating quickly down the street, dragging his suitcase behind him. But I could tell by the way he stared at me, his eyes rolling, searching for recognition, that we actually never made a connection.

Irene Conley's letter came unsolicited, unexpected, in 1989. She had been browsing at an airport bookstore, and her eye had been distracted by a flashy orange and blue dust jacket of a book just recently published about organ transplantation, entitled *Many Sleepless Nights*. When she saw that I was the author, she snatched it off the shelf and read it on the plane to Hawaii, where she was heading for vacation.

What intrigued and surprised her about *Many Sleepless Nights*, she explained, was my interest in health and science and my willingness to discuss issues surrounding death and mortality, subjects I had previously and vigorously avoided. Irene marveled at how the years had changed me. To illustrate, she included a Xeroxed copy of a note I had written after her mother had died in which I attempted to be compassionate but failed miserably. Evidently, I had given her very little support and comfort.

When I saw the copy of this note, I knew for sure that the words and thoughts expressed there were those that had once belonged to me. The phrases, the way in which I put together my sentences, were familiar, as were the self-conscious affectations, an embarrassing habit I adopted as a young writer, such as referring to myself in the third person ("The writer was feeling rather depressed today"), as was Norman Mailer's practice, or omitting articles or personal pronouns in imitation of the spare style of Ernest Hemingway, as in, "Am writing novel. . . . Reads good."

Even my salutation was embarrassingly pretentious. Instead of "Dear Irene," or "Dear Faithful Friend," or even "To whom it may concern," I wrote:

"Yes."

Not even, "Dear Yes." Or "Yes, Irene."

Just: "Yes."

And the paper on which the note was written was from a tablet I had often used. The font was similar to one from an old Adler typewriter I had owned. In fact, although I did not remember the literal act itself, I knew I had composed that letter; it was a vague shadow of distant memory, alive in an unanchored, shifting state deep in my mind.

What I could not remember, however, no matter how hard I tried, was who Irene Conley was. I assumed I had known Irene (or she had known me), judging by the intimate tone of her letter and the fact that she had kept my undated "Yes" note, which is how I began referring to it, for what I guessed to be twenty years. But I had absolutely no recollection, no memory, not the slightest inkling of Irene Conley's identity. Irene may have been part of my history, but I could not conjure up a connection to make her memory real.

I have since wondered if, during those years, I had written "No" letters and notes and "Maybe" letters and notes and "By the way" letters and notes to go along with the "Yes" letters and notes. I have been asking old friends to look through our correspondence for evidence of those or other affectations.

One former student, another Irene, in fact, whom I will call Irene Palladino, actually saved my critiques of her writing, which were carefully typed on my old Adler on the back of eight-by-ten-inch black-and-white photographs of industrial scenes, primarily cement mixers. This was a legacy of my preliterary days when I worked for a large advertising agency that represented various manufacturers of heavy equipment, including a German company specializing in cement mixers. It was my success with this company that led to the Helium Centennial account, which drove me from the advertising and public relations business. But I remember this client especially because, in an effort to call attention to the product, I commissioned a poster with a bikini-clad woman in red Betty Grable spiked-heel ankle-strap shoes draped suggestively on the body of one of their cement mixers. This was the way to attract the attention of contractors and engineers—an inspired idea, it turned out.

We had a party in a hotel to introduce the poster—along with a special appearance from the bikini-clad model. Guests were already very drunk when she walked into the room and began gyrating suggestively. There were hoots and cheers—enthusiastic approval. When the model finished her performance, we all spontaneously, and for no particular reason, flung open the windows and began bombarding pedestrians with whiskey sours from our eleventh-floor suite. Later, I discovered the model snuggled in the bathtub with a purchasing agent for a Midwestern construction company, who soon placed a large order—the beginning of a significant increase in cement mixer sales.

Eventually, after months of frustration, I decided to swallow my pride and deal more directly with the Irene Conley problem. I would write Irene, thanking her for her graciousness concerning *Many Sleepless Nights* and confessing to the inexplicable gap in my memory. Irene might be annoyed, but I assumed she would understand. But when I went back to the file in which I had placed Irene's letter in order to get her address, I suddenly discovered that it was missing. Neither could I find the envelope it was sent in, nor the Xeroxed copy of my "Yes" note that she had also sent me. No matter how hard I looked everything was, suddenly and mysteriously, now gone.

I began suspecting that I had imagined Irene Conley's note and the Xeroxed copy of my letter—that it had not been real—especially in light of my next connection with Irene Palladino, the former student whose work I had critiqued on the back of eight-by-ten-inch photographs of cement mixers. Irene and I had met for a drink and had had a long intimate boozy talk about former friends and lovers. Afterwards I walked her to the subway. She was working in Manhattan at the time and I was in town to visit one of my editors. We paused at the stairs leading down to the trains. I took her in my arms and kissed her.

I recall this moment clearly because I was still married at the time, although it was evident that a divorce was imminent. But to kiss another woman, to taste another's lips, was so unusual, after so long—and delicious. More significant was the fact that this was the first time I had ever kissed a student. I immediately began worrying that I had done something sinful, even though the student in question was a thirty-seven-year-old woman who had not been my student for a decade and a half.

But years later when I reminded Irene Palladino about our romantic early evening encounter in Manhattan, she responded with a raised eyebrow, as if I were joking, and said: "I haven't the slightest idea what you are talking about. The incident you are describing at the subway stairs never happened."

I was flabbergasted. "What do you mean it didn't happen? I can feel it—picture it."

"Can you picture standing on your tiptoes?" she asked. She was referring to the fact that she was considerably taller than I was.

"I was on a step above you," I countered. I couldn't actually recall the details—but that was the way I conceived of it, me standing on the step above her, although suddenly, with Irene's startling information, I was beginning to wonder if I was losing my personal history—not that that was so bad. All my memories aren't sealed with kisses, unfortunately.

But then the situation worsened.

One day in 1995, approximately six years after Irene Conley contacted me, I received a letter from a former student, Pam Shingler.

As she was edging into middle age, she explained, she had decided to contact the people who had affected her life in a negative manner and confront them with what they had done to her. I was the recipient of the first letter she was writing. She told the story of how I was her manuscript-committee chairperson at the University of Pittsburgh while she was a Master of Fine Arts graduate student in creative writing. In our M.F.A. program, a student must take a number of courses in order to earn a graduate creative writing degree and also write a minimum of two hundred "publishable" pages—part of a book project. Committees of three faculty members (one from the literature program, two from creative writing) were formed to help guide the student to a realization of that manuscript goal.

The chairperson of that committee is a major force and influence in the planning and writing of the manuscript, while the other two members serve in a less-involved support capacity. Pam's manuscript was to be a personal narrative about Appalachia, where she grew up. But soon after I approved the concept of her initial chapters, I went on a sabbatical, replaced by a young, pipe-smoking assistant professor who immediately confronted her at their first meeting by attacking her writing style and suggesting that she reconsider the entire project.

When she left his office later that afternoon and stumbled out of the Cathedral of Learning into the cold grayness of the early winter evening, Pam was devastated. She drove back to the small town sixty miles to the north where she had been working and from which she had been commuting and never returned to the university. She also never finished her memoir and soon thereafter abandoned her dream of becoming a writer.

What hurt her most was the fact that she had been attending Pitt on a regular basis for a couple of years, and no one, not my young colleague, not the chair of our department, not even me, when I returned the following year, had ever attempted to find out why she had so suddenly and mysteriously disappeared. With the exception of the invoices and past-due student loan payment notices, no one at the university ever had any contact with her again. Her letter wasn't written with the intent of blaming me, but I was the only person whose name she cared to remember and with whom she had had any sort of relationship. She was settling the score and easing her mind by unloading her burden on me.

When I read her letter, I felt embarrassed and disappointed in myself—but not necessarily because of what had happened to Pam during my absence. Many of our students (the majority, in fact) quit midway through the manuscript-writing process, an ordeal for which most are completely unprepared, preferring to slink off without being reminded of their failures or their inability to continue on with the project that was so massive and beyond them. But what made me feel so embarrassed in this particular situation was the fact that no matter how hard I tried, how much I wracked my brain, I also could not remember who Pam Shingler was. I could not remember one thing about her.

That same week, I received a postcard in the mail. The front of the postcard was a reproduction of a book jacket of a novel entitled *The Virgin Knows*. The back of the postcard contained a blurb from *Publisher's Weekly* praising the novel and the author. Under the blurb was a note penned from the author, Christine Palmedessi Moore, who said simply, "You were the best teacher at Pitt I ever had." Although Pam Shingler had not singled me out for blame, that note might have symbolized a reaffirmation of my teaching effectiveness had it not been for the fact that, as with Pam Shingler and Irene Conley, I also had no recollection of who Christine Palmedessi Moore was. My memory was blank.

I thought back to my encounter with the man I had considered my mentor, Robert Meyers, who had not known who I was when I saw him on the street. I was hurt when Meyers didn't remember me, slighted. Why was I, Lee Gutkind, the muscular former fatty who had once been double his size, the only tenured professor at the University of Pittsburgh without an advanced degree, and the man who was to soon become the Godfather Behind Creative Nonfiction, so fucking forgettable? And what was wrong with my memory—how could I expect others to remember who I was—if I did not recall Irene Conley, Christine Palmedessi Moore, and Pam Shingler, in whose lives I had played such a major role?

Months after I received those two communications—and haunted by my inability to remember these former students—I applied for a travel grant to visit some of the people I had taught, whose careers had taken them on different twists and turns in life. I did not hear from the granting agent for many months. I cannot recall if I forgot about the proposal—or automatically assumed that the silence meant that my proposal was not funded. But many months later, I received a letter saying that my proposal had been granted and that I was to receive enough travel money to see some of the students I had named. When I returned home that day and settled down in my office at my desk to retrieve Christine Palmedessi Moore's postcard and Pam Shingler's letter in order to contact them, I pulled the file into which I had thrown them out of the drawer and there, under the file on the bottom of the drawer, suddenly, staring me in the face after a six-year absence, was the missing letter from Irene Conley, along with the Xeroxed copy of the note that I had written to her when her mother died and the envelope with her return address.

I was stunned by this development. I was not a believer in the magic of coincidence other than the fact that coincidences do happen from time to time. I usually didn't read anything deeper into such happenings. But how could I not, in this case, after suddenly receiving a grant I had long ago given up on, and then on the same day discovering a note that had inspired me to write the grant proposal that had been missing for nearly six years?

It took me three months to finally sit down and write Irene Conley a letter, telling her I would like to see her and apologizing for the six-year gap since her nice note to me about my book. I didn't mention, of course, that I couldn't remember who she was. I still hadn't the slightest recollection. I just told her truthfully that I had misplaced her note and then luckily rediscovered it. Now I told her I would be in California for a business meeting and wanted to stop and see her. A few weeks later, I received a one-sentence, one-line return note, telling me that her life was a zoo but that she would welcome the chance to become reacquainted after so long. I made my plans to visit Oakland, California, where she lived, along with some other destinations for later that summer, and eventually made my way west.

Now, I was driving from Santa Cruz through San Jose on Highway 17, on my way to see and/or meet the mysterious Irene Conley. I was very excited—and apprehensive.

Since trading notes some weeks ago, we had had two brief telephone conversations, both very businesslike, having to do with determining a time, day, and place to meet. I learned that she now operated her own day-care center in Oakland. First she said that finding help to carve out time for us to talk would be difficult. But then she began reserving more of my time. Our initial plan to meet for dinner at her house was now extended to include lunch and subsequently the entire afternoon prior to dinner with family and friends.

As I neared the outskirts of Oakland and saw the exit to the famed Jack London Square from Highway 17, I realized I would have to be spending an inordinate amount of time with this woman, and I was filled with trepidation. What happens if I don't like her or if in fact I don't even know her? Perhaps she had written to the wrong person, a different Lee. Throughout the weeks leading up to this fast-approaching moment, I had felt certain I would eventually run into someone who could enlighten me as to Irene's true identity, or that I would see or remember something that would trigger recognition in my own mind. Neither situation occurred. But as I began looking for a parking space for my rental car, I felt fairly confident that I would remember her true identity and make a connection to our past, the moment I laid eyes on her. I parked my car and entered Jack London Square through the back way.

On the telephone the night before, Irene had described the way in which the square was laid out. Her voice was not familiar. We had decided to meet at the large Barnes and Noble Bookstore at the edge of the square in an area in which people sat in the sun near a fountain or at tables, drinking coffee. I entered through the rear doorway and walked down a few narrow book-lined corridors to reach the men's room in order to wash my face and hands. I then reemerged through the side door, intending to catch a glimpse of Irene before she saw me. I hoped to instantly recapture her identity the moment I saw her.

Unfortunately I couldn't see much of what was going on outside through the window from the inside, and my hopes were further dashed when I stepped out into the sunny eating area behind Jack London Square. It was mostly empty at that time of day and those few women sitting alone at tables did not look up when I entered and were clearly disinterested in me as I passed. I did note a woman sitting by the fountain at the far end of the eating area, watching me closely. I examined her through my sunglasses, hoping that I would recognize a familiar Irene face, which would reveal her identity.

As I eased my way tentatively in her direction, she stood up and started to walk toward me. When I hesitated, she began to move more quickly. When I stopped, she was running toward me. Suddenly, we were in each other's arms, and she was kissing and hugging me, saying how happy she was that we could finally get back together. When I managed to ease myself out of her arms and back away slightly so that I could see what Irene Conley looked like close up, I realized that I had never seen this woman before in my entire life.

We sat down at the fountain to look at one another. She kept shaking her head from side to side and repeating. "So good to see you. So good to see you. Such a long time."

I nodded, shook my head up and down and tried to smile warmly, as if I too was breathlessly happy.

"For God's sake. A long time!" she squealed.

"Positively incredible," I said.

"You are such an eyeful to behold," she said.

"And you," I replied. "My friend . . . Irene."

This was the only course of action I could think of: to continue the charade of knowing her and being overwhelmed to see her and to draw out the conversation until such time as a light bulb of recognition was illuminated—or until I felt comfortable enough to come clean with the truth, which was that I didn't know who in the hell she was and that I could not remember one fragment of detail from our past relationship. The only thing that she had said to help narrow her identity was in her initial exclamation when we first embraced. "Thirty years. It's been thirty years."

This was significant. My life had changed a great deal during the past thirty years and most of the people who were my friends then are not friends now. But wouldn't I remember someone with whom I had been so close, even though thirty years had gone by? Obviously not.

"Well, shall we get a cup of coffee?" I asked her.

"Coffee, hell," she replied. "I want a beer." And then she said: "What about our Reuben sandwiches? Do you still like Reuben sandwiches? God," she said, shaking her head and groaning with ecstasy. "I will never forget those incredible Reubens we shared and how much you loved them."

While it was true that I had eaten Reuben sandwiches here and there throughout my life, I do not remember having a special passion for Reubens, especially in Pittsburgh where we had allegedly known each other, and hardly a Mecca for kosher-style deli food. But once again, I felt I should follow her cues for the time being. "Sure. I love Reuben sandwiches," I said.

"Well," she said, "there's a place in this town known to make the best Reubens in the world. I thought of you and your Reuben fixation as soon as I heard about it when I first moved here."

We took off down the street in search of the Reuben restaurant, talking more of my travels in California the past couple of weeks, the highway between Santa Cruz, where I had started this morning, and Jack London Square now, four hours later. In a few minutes, we discovered that the Reuben sandwich Mecca she had been touting had been taken over by a TGI Friday's, so we returned to the square, where she pointed out important landmarks, including a train stop and the benches, which tomorrow would be the lunchtime site of the children enrolled in her day-care center. We looked at the Jack London statue and read aloud the plaque that celebrated his life, strolled over to Jack London's log cabin, dismantled from its original site in Alaska and reconstructed here and went into an old bar with slanted floors and Jack London memorabilia, said to have been frequented by the author.

Later, standing in front of that bar, I stopped a passerby and asked if she would snap a picture of Irene and me. During this time— perhaps forty-five minutes or an hour had passed—I probed her with questions in a gentle but persistent way, seeking recognition, looking for a connection, a mutual friend, a regular hang-out— some way to place Irene Conley in the complicated spectrum of my life. But the people she named were unrecognizable. She had not lived in the neighborhood in which I had grown up, nor the neighborhood I had taken for my home and where I have lived through most of my adult life. She had not been my student nor known me as a teacher. The fact that I rode a motorcycle for many years and that my first book was about my experiences traveling the United States on a two-wheeled machine was news to her; my second book, about major league baseball umpires, didn't ring a bell, either.

We found a restaurant, sat down, and ordered a beer and lunch. Meanwhile, I continued to ask leading questions, while offering information from my life history that would enable her to make connections. I was becoming increasingly dismayed that I couldn't place her in my life. Was this my first sign of senility—Alzheimer's? There wasn't a doubt in her mind that we had been (were still) very close. She remembered more about me than I remembered about myself. Or was this a bizarre hoax? Was Irene a serial killer and I the object of her obsession?

Irene said that we had met at Pitt in a Shakespeare class sometime during the late 1960s, but to my recollection I had never taken a Shakespeare class at the University of Pittsburgh or anywhere else. I asked her the name of the professor. She could not remember. I then named all of the professors with whom I remembered studying, including Robert Meyers. She recognized not one name. She did have the timespan in which I attended college correctly placed however, the late 1960s, but that was all.

I peered at her across the table. Her face, wrinkled and puffy, meant nothing to me. Her hair was straight and almost white, and she had a very strange gaze, off-center, that hinted a lack of focus. She couldn't seem to look directly into my eyes, and she slurred some of her words as if she were slightly inebriated, or on a psychotropic medication. Irene was heavy-set, egg-shaped, casual, in a sweatshirt, canvas shoes, and baggy, wrinkled pants. "Oh, don't look so intensely at me," she nearly shrieked. "I've aged so badly. As you know, my life has been difficult."

I nodded sympathetically, as if I did indeed understand. "I'm sorry," I said.

Now it was her turn to talk and catch me up on what had happened since we were last together. In Pittsburgh, she had a legal battle with her husband for the custody of their two children. She first returned to Buffalo, New York, her hometown, to care for her dying mother. This was the incident to which I referred in the note I wrote, which she had duplicated and returned to me, when I had apologized for my lack of compassion and empathy. I had evidently not paid much attention at the time. After her mother died, she went to San Francisco, where the rest of the flower children were, but then moved to Oakland, where she lived on welfare with her kids for a while in the ghetto, got a job as an aide at a neighborhood day-care center, and began rebuilding her life. A few years later, she met Alan, her second husband, an engineer who owned an electrical supply business. She worked in Alan's business, but eventually convinced him to help her start her own day-care center, which has turned out to be a successful venture.

Irene was knowledgeable and enthusiastic about her work, although I had a hard time imagining this odd-looking, out-of-focus woman as the leader of a day-care center to which I might entrust my son. But as I began sipping my second beer, I felt increasingly relaxed, giving myself to the conversation as if I were actually catching up with a long-lost friend. I outlined the sordid details surrounding both of my marriages, my subsequent divorces, and the losses and humiliations I had endured. My bad luck in love was pale compared to the tragedies Irene had endured. Alan was dying from leukemia. "If he acts strange," she said, "remember that he's very tense. He gets through life by working hard during the day and drinking hard at night. I don't like him when he's drunk, but it's what he needs to do to get by." Her older son, who might show up for dinner, had a brain tumor and was also dying. Her youngest daughter, a biracial adopted baby, suffered from elephant man's disease and was mentally handicapped. Her other daughter lived in another city with an illegitimate child.

"It's been tough going," Irene said, shaking her head and laughing.

"You've been through the mill," I said.

We were now finished eating, three beers later. I paid the check. We walked to her car, a tiny Mazda Miata, to which she referred as "my pride and joy." She drove me to my rental car and I followed her to her house in Piedmont on the Oakland-Piedmont line, a middle-class neighborhood and house, smallish in size and well kept up on the outside. As she warned me and I was soon to discover, her strong point was not housekeeping. Litter boxes for her cats were scattered about the house, as were grains of the litter on the carpet and in the kitchen. The bathroom and the kitchen were clean, although the telephone was caked with years of filth.

I sat down and the dialogue continued. Even though I was convinced I didn't know her, all of my inhibitions had disappeared. I was very comfortable. We talked for at least an hour. "Wait," she said. "I know what this party needs." She went into the kitchen, then immediately returned with a bottle of liqueur, Cherry Kijafa. "You'll meet Tim tonight at dinner. I met him in Buffalo right after you abandoned me."

"I what?" I said.

"While my mom was dying," she answered.

"Oh yeah," I replied. "I can't apologize enough . . . I'm so sorry."

"You did the best you could do," Irene said. "Your note explained it. Anyway, I met Tim, and he sat with me by mom's bed in the hospital every night. And do you know what we did?"

"No. What?"

"We drank Cherry Kijafa and talked about you."

"You talked about me?" I asked.

"I was angry at you at the time," she said. "Tim calmed me down."

From midafternoon when she opened the bottle until dinner that night at 7:30 or 8:00 P.M., Irene drank steadily from the Cherry Kijafa bottle until it was mostly empty. She had been planning to take me over to her day-care center to meet the kids and see the facilities, but she said that she was uncomfortable driving while drinking and there was nothing to see without the kids there, anyway; the kids were gone at that point.

Alan, a short pudgy man with intense and jerky mannerisms, arrived home. After shaking my hand and pumping my arm with great enthusiasm and telling me how delighted he was to meet "the real Lee Gutkind" after hearing about him for all of these years, he disappeared into the kitchen to drink beer and prepare dinner. When Tim arrived for drinks at 6:30 and Irene poured him a glass of Kijafa, she said, "Tim, remember how many of these bottles we shared in Buffalo when my mother was dying and Lee had abandoned me?"

And Tim, a slight, short man in his late forties, who was a hospital administrator, wrinkled his brows and shook his head. "I can't ever remember drinking Cherry Kijafa before."

At 7:00, Kay, a tall, middle-aged black woman, arrived. According to Irene, Kay had invited herself to the dinner when she learned that I was to be the guest of honor. "Irene has talked about you for years," Kay laughed and wagged her finger. "The things I know about you . . ."

"What do you know?" I asked rather sharply, desperately seeking any straw that would connect me with Irene in a way that I could understand.

"Oh, I'll never tell," Kay replied. "But Irene has read many of your books. She tells us about everything you write."

Kay sipped from a glass of Cherry Kijafa and told a long, fascinating story about her eldest son, a teenager with serious behavioral problems. Last summer he drank a quart of gin while smoking four joints, then tumbled backwards from a second floor balcony and toppled end-over-end like a football to the sidewalk. Although she had threatened repeatedly that if he had gotten into any more trouble she would not allow him back into the house, Kay cared for him during a long recovery and rehabilitation, knowing that something had to happen, something had to be done to change his behaviors or he would eventually end up killing himself.

One day listening to the radio, she heard an announcement about a home for elderly homeless men and, the following morning, went to see the director. Kay realized that as long as her son interacted with people his own age, exclusively, he would continue to find ways of getting into trouble, "He needed to be with people who could teach him something—not antagonize and test him. I figured those old down-and-out men could talk with him about the decisions they had made that brought them to this point of poverty and despair." In the year since he had moved into the shelter, and despite a series of setbacks early on, her son seemed more settled, much less vulnerable to peer pressure and, most importantly, had found some sense of peace with God.

As Kay told her story, Tim and Irene interjected anecdotes and details that Kay had forgotten. Evidently, Kay and Irene met when Irene first came to Oakland and had gotten involved in the local day-care center. Tim had followed Irene to northern California from Buffalo. A few years ago, Kay was a victim of breast cancer. Her mastectomy took place in the hospital where Tim worked. The night of her mastectomy, Alan, Irene, and Tim shared the waiting room.

Meanwhile, as we were all talking, and the sun outside dipped lower into the sky, Alan, who had been feverishly preparing our dinner, would dash in his frantic, intense way out of the kitchen, through the dining room and living room, fling open the front door and disappear outside. Then, after a few minutes, he would return, in a much more sedate fashion, and walk back through the living room and into the kitchen to continue dinner preparations. This occurred at least a half-dozen times during Kijafa and conversation, but no one, except for me, seemed to notice.

Now Irene looked at her watch, jumped up, and ran toward the television in the corner of the living room. "Wait! It's time for

Hillary." This was the night Hillary Clinton was to address the Democratic National Convention. But just at that moment, Alan stepped into the living room and said, "Dinner is served."

"It has to be postponed," Irene said to Alan.

"But the food will get cold . . ." said Alan.

"Hillary will heat it up," said Kay.

Alan relented. As Hillary talked, Alan dashed frantically from his kitchen, trying to keep our food warm, and out the front door, returning a few minutes later, as usual, with a much slower, calmer demeanor. But at the very end of Hillary's talk—we were actually sitting back and taking in the applause, while Tim and Kay and Irene were clapping and cheering—Alan suddenly burst into the room. "It's here! It's here!" he yelled.

Now, everybody jumped up, abandoning Hillary, and chased Alan outside in the dark. I followed the group down the front steps and into the middle of the street, where Alan was standing like a statue pointing up at the sky. Unbeknownst to me, Alan had been seeking the Russian Mir satellite, launched earlier that month, which, according to the newspaper, would be visible from the Oakland-Piedmont section of the city at sundown. Alan had been waiting for this moment.

Tonight was the perfect clear night for the Mir to be spied. The Mir came across the darkened sky in a narrow, yellow line, cutting the horizon in half. It could not have been mistaken for anything else but a satellite because of its constant, unchanging illumination and its very sure, straight path. We stood in the middle of the street, noisily marveling at the Mir until it faded from the sky. Then we went back inside to a dinner, which was now cold and not as tasty as Alan had meant it to be.

But listening to Kay's story and Hillary Clinton's presentation, spotting Alan's Mir streak soundlessly through the sky, hearing Irene's nonstop commentary about our entangled relationship, all served to make the dinner ambiance warm and comfortably intimate. As the *pièce de résistance*, Irene had purchased a bottle of a wine she and I had allegedly drunk together at our many dinners thirty years ago in Pittsburgh—Matuse, a sparking rosé. Indeed I remembered drinking great quantities of Matuse during my hippie days, although none with Irene. Even now, nothing in my vast catalog of recollections could yet forge any connection with Irene Conley.

Our conversation during dinner hopped, skipped, and jumped from the topics I had chosen for my later books, such as organ transplantation and children with mental health problems, to stories about Kay's son and Irene's day-care work. Not counting me, here were four people who loved one another and enjoyed each other's company, but did not see one another as much as they might have wanted to. I was happy to have brought them together, even though I hadn't the slightest idea how it had happened.

As the evening came to an end, we all realized how well we had bonded; we were drinking Matuse and celebrating one another's lives. Irene and I toasted each other as old friends reunited, and then everyone drank more wine to our pledge of keeping our newfound connection alive. Then Alan announced that he may be in remission; his most recent tests showed that he was not getting any worse which, he pointed out, meant that he could live significantly longer than he had expected. Then Kay said that she and her son were now attending church together and that they were discovering a sense of salvation and rebirth in Christianity. Tim said he was getting a promotion. We talked a lot about faith during those last few minutes we were together and how the newest scientific studies seem to indicate that sick people who are prayed for by friends and family get better faster than people who aren't prayed for by others. We all promised to pray for Alan.

It was time to leave. Nine hours had passed since I had first met Irene Conley at Jack London Square. I had dreaded those nine hours the moment I laid eyes on this perfect stranger, but the time had gone by in a delightful and therapeutic flash. I shook hands with Alan and Tim and put Kay's big hand in mine and squeezed it. And then I embraced Irene Conley and thanked her for opening up her home and her life to me. "However long we will be apart, and until we next meet, you will always be a member of my family," she said.

Later, to Kay, Alan, and Tim, I sent copies of books I had written that they had requested. I wrote a long letter to Irene Conley, reiterating my thanks for connecting me to her friends and opening up her heart to me. But curiously, I have never heard from Tim, Kay, Alan, or Irene Conley since our evening together, fours years ago. Recently, when in San Francisco, I tried to telephone Irene at home and at the day-care center she owned. Both numbers had been disconnected.

Low-Clearance Story

Sam was obsessed with my low-clearance stories. I told him these stories three or four times a day, on request. His two favorites were the "flood" low-clearance story and the "motorcycle" low-clearance story. I always told the flood low-clearance story first. It began with me driving on a country road, on my way to see a potential client, when a downpour started. I was a representative for a shoe manufacturer at the time—a traveling salesman. This was my first job after leaving the military and before entering college.

"When the rain ended, the roads were covered with mud," I would tell him. "I drove carefully until I reached an underpass below a bridge, flooded by a nearby creek. I admit I should have turned around—the water was at least two feet high—but instead I decided to be daring and edge my way through it. When I saw water seeping through the floorboards, I realized my mistake. Soon, my car began to cough and sputter; it died quietly, stranding me in the middle of a small lake. I took off my shoes and socks, rolled up my trousers, waded to dry ground and sat down, hoping someone would show up to help. I only had to wait a few minutes until a man in a tow truck happened by, a lucky coincidence. He said he had been dispatched on another call, but agreed to make a quick stop and pull my car out of the water. 'This will only take a minute,' he said. He ground his truck into gear—it was a Ford—and much higher off the road than my car, obviously . . . *too* high . . . because as soon as he pulled under the underpass, we heard this sickening scraping noise. Then suddenly, his truck stopped dead in the middle of the water. The tow bar was stuck against the top of the bridge; the truck was wedged in—could not move one inch in any direction."

The motorcycle low-clearance story was similar to the flood low-clearance story, although this story took place at a time when I did not own a car and I traveled everywhere on a big black BMW motorcycle. I wore a leather jacket, tight-fitting leather pants and big black boots with heavy metal cleats on the heel and toe. " 'The Cleat' was my nickname—what people called me," I explained to Sam. "When I walked around Shadyside, which was the neighborhood where I hung out, friends anticipated my arrival by listening for the distant clumping sound of my cleats."

The morning the story took place was just like any other. I walked out to the garage to start up my motorcycle. At this point in the story, I would often raise my foot as high as I could and then kick down on the ground a couple of times, simulating a kick start, until Sam responded by yelling, "Vroom, Vroom, Vroom."

"Then I got on my bike, coasted down the drive, and took off up the street," I would continue, all the while simulating the sound and movement of the motorcycle advancing through the gears. "But I discovered that Ellsworth Avenue, a key artery, was suddenly enmeshed in a horrible traffic jam. Luckily, on a motorcycle you can weave your way in and out of cars in traffic jams, which I did. Until I saw what was causing all of the trouble."

It was a gigantic tractor-trailer truck. "The driver had ventured into the underpass below the Ellsworth Avenue Bridge and got stuck. The top of the trailer was wedged up against the bottom of the bridge, just like the driver of the tow truck had gotten wedged in the underpass while helping to retrieve my flooded car. By the time I arrived on my cycle, the tractor-trailer truck driver was shifting back and forth, gear to gear, gunning his engine, forward and reverse—but wasn't moving an inch in either direction. He was frustrated and embarrassed. Stranded motorists were yelling and screaming, calling him names. There must have been 150 cars backed up, and the line was getting longer and louder by the minute. I decided to try to help."

So, at this point, the flood low-clearance story and the motorcycle low-clearance stories converge, a place and time in the narratives that has always allowed me to say something to Sam about what he might learn from these stories. This is what I do both as a father in the process of raising my son and as a creative nonfiction writer. I will first try to engage Sam—and my reader—with stories he finds interesting and compelling. Later, I will embed these stories with information, so that Sam (or my readers) will learn about motorcycles, traffic patterns, and so on. Finally, I try to infuse these stories with moral or meaning. Everyone is interested in finding wisdom and direction in events that happen to them and to the people they know. Coincidence and similarity provide a special appeal. So, using those life experiences, I teach my readers—and, most importantly, Sam.

In the flood low-clearance story, a primary objective is to illustrate the virtues of being gracious and helping people in need. The tow-truck driver plowed through the high water because I, a stranger, needed help. True, he should have been more cautious and thoughtful about his good deed—which is another life lesson Sam can learn: to think before taking action when possible and to evaluate in advance the potential consequences of whatever action he eventually chooses. Which leads to the third life lesson for Sam: to be secure enough to remain composed when a decision does not work out. The motorcycle low-clearance story is a version of the golden rule—reaching out to help others (a trucker in this case), just as a trucker once tried to help me. It is also an example of how the importance of maintaining a clear vision of your predicament can save the day.

At a key point in both stories, we hear the wailing police siren and then see the flashing red light. In the flood low-clearance story, a Pennsylvania state trooper with his crisp, gray uniform and wide-brimmed Smokey-the-Bear hat arrives on the scene, and in the motorcycle low-clearance story, the Pittsburgh police officer is wearing dark blue, trimmed with gold, and is a bit more rumpled. They climb out of their vehicles, slam their doors, and stomp over to the truckers, who quickly explain the embarrassing difficulty, their rigs wedged in between the bottom of the bridge and the road.

The trooper and the policeman are similarly angry—nearly fuming at the unnecessary stupidity of the situations with which they must deal. They get right to the point. "I want to ask you an important question," they bark at the truckers. "How high is your truck?"

This is something most truckers would know instantly—and they do know. "Twelve feet, eight inches," the tractor-trailer truck driver answers from the seat of his truck. "Ten feet, two inches," the tow-truck driver announces, knee-deep in the muddy water.

Then the police officers lift their forefingers in an authoritative manner and slowly crook them back and forth in a silent but threatening "come with me" kind of gesture. The truckers follow the police officers over to the front of the underpass and, with the same forefingers, the officers point upward at the sign posted above the entrance. There is then a dramatic pause as the truckers look up in the appropriate direction, at which point both react with immediate dismay. "And do you know what the sign posted at the entrance to the underpass said?" I will sometimes ask Sam, to make sure I have his undivided attention.

"LOW CLEARANCE! It is LOW CLEARANCE: TWELVE FEET FIVE INCHES for the Ellsworth Avenue Bridge and LOW CLEARANCE: TEN FEET for the flood underpass," he will scream.

"And what does this mean, Sam?"

"It means that these two truck drivers are not too smart!"

In both low-clearance stories, the truckers are portrayed as ineffectual and slow-witted, while I come off looking pretty good, a father for Sam to be proud of. In both my salesman and my motorcycle personae, I display a quiet intelligence, helping to make peace between all parties. In the flood low-clearance story, I climb onto the truck and hang onto the end of the tow bar, allowing the force of my weight to disengage the bar from the top of the underpass, while the trucker slowly edges his vehicle forward. "This wasn't brain surgery," I tell Sam. "But it was the obvious thing to do—and it worked." In the motorcycle low-clearance story, I go from the top of the tow truck to the bottom of the tractor-trailer truck and let air out of the tires to allow it enough clearance to set itself free. But in both cases my good deed is only half done.

I bring resolution to the conflict between the trooper and the trucker by suggesting that the driving rain may have caused a tree branch to temporarily conceal the low-clearance sign. In the motorcycle low-clearance story, I convinced the police officer (I persuaded him to sit in the cab of the truck) that the low-clearance sign was placed in such a way that observation from certain angles was nearly impossible. (This required a lot of stretching and leaning, along with a little seat manipulation—but it worked.)

In addition to engaging Sam and allowing me to teach a few life lessons, the low-clearance stories also enable me to tell Sam more about who and what I was—a person he will never know—during the 1970s. Right now, my professional strengths as a teacher and writer are fairly inaccessible to Sam; he sees me writing in my office at home and views the final product—books about subjects he can't quite relate to—with a polite distance. Once in a while, I will take him to class with me, but he is much too involved in the books he is reading or my laptop computer, which he covets, and hardly pays attention to my teaching style or how students respond to me. This is often frustrating because I want Sam to be proud of his dad and, if not as engaged in my life as I am in his, at least aware of my professional and personal assets.

But usually I can't impress him with the things I do best. He is not interested in sports, for example, so my knowledge of baseball history or passion for cars and motorcycles are of no use. Sam is attuned to computers and scientific subjects. He reads a great deal; he loves manuals—appliances, cell phones, sound systems, and a range of gadgets. I, on the other hand, have little patience for electrical and mechanical objects. I don't care how they work; rather I want them to function flawlessly. When they fail, I immediately discard them: toasters, tape recorders, microwave ovens are in my trash bin the moment they act up. Furthermore, Sam and I don't work out or play ball together, first, because he is not interested in sports and second, because my own recreational interests—running mostly or pumping the Stairmaster or skiing the Nordic Track—are solitary. We did have one physical activity that we enjoyed doing together: bicycling—at least until recently.

Sam adjusted to biking early and became a skillful and fearless two-wheeler. Last summer, we took a number of five- and six-mile trips, winding through the neighborhood, stopping for lunch at his favorite spot, The Pita Garden, for grilled American cheese on pita bread and chocolate milk. For Christmas, I bought him a sophisticated bike with six gears so that we could take longer and more challenging trips. Then Sam suddenly lost interest, refusing to bike throughout the spring and early summer—a development that profoundly saddened and perplexed me. Although I refused to admit culpability, I knew in my heart that his rejection of biking was my fault, a direct rebuke to my parenting philosophy and style of life. I am, as Patricia says, "disgustingly overbearing."

Truly, I do not consider myself an especially bright or talented person. My strengths as a writer relate directly to my ability to focus on an idea and objective and stick to it, no matter how much time or effort it requires, until I achieve my goal. I get up at 4:30 A.M. seven days a week, holidays and vacations included, and I write for sometimes eight or ten hours a day, refusing to relent until I've produced a page or two that I truly feel has potential—and then I write those pages again the following morning and often many mornings after that.

After losing weight and slimming down in the military, I began running marathons. I've completed four Outward Bound wilderness expeditions with rock climbing, solo survival, and other character-testing challenges. More challenging was psychotherapy, twice a week, with a neo-Freudian analyst for nine years. This all resonates with my Winston Churchill "never give up . . . never, ever, ever give up" and "fall down nine times . . . get up ten" sloganeering, so irritating to Patricia—and others.

I don't claim to live up to these philosophical platitudes every day of my life. But I am constantly pushing everyone I know to do more than they want to do. Wherever we went on any of our vacations, Patricia now tells me, I always wanted to walk one more mile or see one more monument; whenever we worked on remodeling the house, I always forced her to work one more hour, then one more hour after that. I expect people to invest themselves into whatever activity they are attempting and to try as hard as possible to achieve the ultimate reward. It is not worthwhile to do anything halfway, which may be true for me but, as I am continuing to learn, not true for others, including Sam.

Over the past year, Sam and I had peddled Beechwood Boulevard, a gradual mile-long grade with a couple of deep dips, a half-dozen times. Sometimes Sam would stop and walk when the hill became too much for him. But I had discovered that by offering him extra time at the computer I could inspire him to continue to ride—without rest—to the top. More rewarding than the computer time was the ecstasy Sam experienced whenever he achieved the summit; his smile enveloped his face. So it was only natural for me, after witnessing these successes a couple of times, that I build in one more hill to the Beechwood Boulevard route—scene of his triumph. This was only a small hill—perhaps no more than a city block long—but I knew immediately, glancing at Sam's face, that I had made the wrong decision. I had pushed him a tad too far—and he snapped. No more than ten yards into that final hill, Sam stopped peddling and dropped his bike to the ground. "I am not going any further," he said simply. "I quit." I pushed his bike to the top of the hill and eventually convinced him to ride home downhill, but I knew by the look on his face and the tension between us that the comfort and camaraderie that had previously existed when we biked together might not be duplicated in the near future. I had done my best, but I had made a calculated mistake. We stopped riding completely for about a month. I thought that some time could and should pass before biking together again; I was looking forward to an upcoming trip to Atlantic City for a wedding, hoping that the famous Boardwalk would rekindle Sam's biking interest.

I had recently purchased a bike rack for my Ford Explorer; with the bike rack mounted on top of the roof rack, it was so high that I needed a small stepladder to lock the bikes on top. There are four tunnels along the Pennsylvania Turnpike from Pittsburgh to Philadelphia, and that day on our way to Atlantic City, Sam and I had a terrific time speculating about the low-clearance limits for each of them and the likelihood that we would make it to New Jersey with our bikes and roof rack intact. Interestingly, we were unable to locate low-clearance warning signs at the entrances to the tunnels, but hours later, I clearly saw the sign hanging on a chain suspended from the ceiling as I entered the Atlantic City Holiday Inn parking garage—LOW CLEARANCE: SIX FEET EIGHT INCHES—and I immediately ignored it, thinking that the posted clearance seemed unnecessarily low. I figured I could easily drive up the ramp without incident. And I almost did. The Explorer cruised untouched from the first to the second level—until we collided loudly, sickeningly, with two ceiling pipes that I had believed I could slip under. I stopped the car, took a deep breath, closed my eyes, counted to ten—and then when I suddenly realized the impact of what I had done—the ironic meaning based on all of my low-clearance stories and clever life lessons I had force-fed to Sam, I totally lost my composure. I began punching the steering wheel and yelling "Stupid! Stupid! Stupid!" Even as I was in the middle of my tantrum, I couldn't believe that I was acting so foolishly, but I literally couldn't help myself.

I jumped out of the car to inspect the damage. The pipe had sliced my bike's seat in half. I felt lucky. Bike seats were inexpensive, relatively—and, most importantly, *Sam's* bike was untouched. At that point, I was so embarrassed that I had displayed such poor judgment in front of Sam, and then had lost most of my composure, that I just wanted to get the experience over with. Maybe take a swim in the ocean and redeem myself in my son's eyes. And I wanted to demonstrate that my judgment wasn't that faulty and that I had made just one tiny miscalculation and that in the end everything would be all right. It was only a ruined bike seat, after all. Daddy's bike seat—not Sam's.

So, quite hurriedly, without looking for any additional obstruction, I jumped back into the Explorer, started the engine, put it into gear, stomped on the accelerator—and immediately smashed into another water pipe—the last remaining pipe between me and the top. Now both bikes clattered to the ground and the water pipe with which I had collided was torn from its anchor on the ceiling. It was bending precariously, as if it were about to break and burst. I paused to assess the situation—and to take a deep breath. I tried to imagine what Winston Churchill might do at a moment like this or how he would advise his people. But this had nothing to do with tenacity or dedication; it had much more to do with humility and self-respect—or the sudden lack or it. I wanted so much to be able to escape the embarrassment of the situation in front of Sam and to survive with some dignity, but instead of rallying to the moment, falling down nine times and getting up ten, I suddenly, in defiance of whatever dignity I had remaining, began to cry. And when I felt the heat of the tears in my eyes, I began punching the steering wheel one more time and I heard myself yelling even louder than the first time, "Stupid! Stupid! Stupid!" Sitting in that car, punching the steering wheel, yelling and screaming and feeling nakedly foolish in front of my son, I remember thinking, "This is the worst moment of my life."

But unfortunately this wasn't the worst moment of my life. In fact, this wasn't even the worst moment of my weekend. The Atlantic City low-clearance story went from bad to worse, as far as bicycling and my father-son relationship with Sam was concerned. I fixed Sam's bike in the parking garage later that afternoon—while a borrowed roll of duct tape temporarily secured my seat—thinking that Sam and I would be able to bike ride together, as planned. But the following day when I told Sam it was time to get ready to ride, he declined. And the next day when I brought the subject up, he declined again. When I finally persuaded him to bike the Boardwalk later that week, he ran out of gas almost immediately and began to cry—until I agreed to quit.

From that point on and through the rest of our vacation in New Jersey, Sam virtually ignored me. Suddenly, he didn't want to go biking anymore—for the "foreseeable future," he said. And he didn't trust me to take him into the water by myself. He didn't want me to make him breakfast, to put him on my shoulders and walk, or drive in the car with me, if a second car and another driver were available. I probably should have given him some space—ignored the situation and gradually allowed it to fade from memory. But contrary to what I knew to be the best course of action, it would be fair to say that I handled this situation inappropriately at every opportunity, exhibiting an incredible lack of parental wisdom and adultlike restraint. I complained. I yelled. I threatened. I moped. I beseeched him to explain what was going on between us, what I had done to deserve such a sudden freeze-out of affection. At home, I was Mr. Mom. I was in charge of the care and affection of Sam from morning until dinner. His mother helped out regularly, but basically I have been the most dominant parent.

Patricia was another witness to my Atlantic City situation, having driven up with us from Pittsburgh in the Explorer. Despite being divorced, we had successfully maintained a relationship of sorts, based on our mutual responsibilities to Sam. In fact, in a very unorthodox shared-custody arrangement, Patricia and I were next-door neighbors; Sam could dash back and forth across a small brick courtyard and switch from mother to father, bedroom to bedroom, toy to toy, whenever he wanted. To her credit, Patricia had kept a low profile in the car through all of these events and didn't say what she was probably thinking about how I couldn't even drive or judge distances without her and how relieved she was to have dumped me and sandbagged our marriage when she did. But I don't think she was blameless, either. The fact is, her presence is constantly intimidating to me; she is living proof that I have been less than desired as a husband or a man. When we had first gotten married, the shoe was on the other foot; she admired and attempted to emulate all of my qualities, most especially the way in which I worked hard to achieve my goals, no matter how elusive they might have been.

Early into our relationship, Patricia had elucidated her own goals, which, from her point of view, were formidable. All the people we knew were college educated; many of my colleagues had Ph.D.'s. She wanted an education, but was paralyzed with fright that she would fail. Because I knew that she wanted me on some level to help her, I shouldered her burden with her. I helped her select a program, after examining the offerings of many colleges in the area, and register for classes. I provided the wherewithal for her to buy a car and commute to a distant campus. But more than anything I became her coach and the moral equivalent of her conscience. Every time she backslid through math or chemistry or calculus— she was working toward a B.S.N. degree—I cheered her onward, literally intimidating her with my Winston Churchill, "fall down nine times, get up ten" rhetoric and my own very large presence. I could not tutor Patricia, but because of my own forcefulness and conviction and refusal to falter, I could give her the strength to endure difficult challenges and achieve her goals.

In the end, Patricia did succeed by earning her degree and obtaining a very good job as a researcher in a large medical facility. I was the loser, for I had imposed myself upon her in the most unbearable of ways, and she had come to recognize in me the most negative and unflattering qualities. I know that she appreciated my help and support—and loved me for it on a certain level—but she had completely overdosed on me at the same time. I guess I had done my job as a coach and conscience too well; I was much too much like a parent or teacher; I could never again be her lover or, perhaps even, her intimate friend.

Meanwhile, with all of our history running through my head during our Atlantic City vacation, I was becoming paranoid. Sam was comparing his two parents, I imagined: his cool, elegant mother, flipping through *New Yorker* and *Esquire* magazines in the back seat of the car and his father, a tottering middle-aged, uncoordinated bozo with a low-clearance hero-fantasy. The fact that I am one of those midlife fathers—Sam wasn't born until I was in my forties— always makes me feel that everything I do as a father has got to be right because I may not have a second chance to do it again.

Was he giving up on me, I wondered, because my judgment and behavior in the parking garage had been so inappropriate—and was in vivid contrast to the strong, thoughtful male figure I represented in the motorcycle and flood low-clearance stories? Patricia gave up on me, didn't she? Walking away from a person who, she admitted, had always tried to be a good husband. Maybe Sam, like his mother, had lost faith in his father. Maybe I had stretched the limits of believability too far, allowed my imagination to run away in the process of telling and retelling the low-clearance stories I thought Sam loved so much. More likely, I was just being my true overbearing self—the real Lee Gutkind at his best, which was also my disgusting and obnoxious worst. Mr. "Fall down nine times, get up ten." Mr. "One more hill." Mr. "One more hour." Wracked with guilt and insecurity, I feared that my son no longer appreciated his daddy, if he ever did, and was totally fixated on mother, who preferred swimming and making sand castles to biking and hard work and high-level achievement. I fell into a terrible funk for the rest of the trip. I felt just the way I imagined my father felt when he contemplated me, hanging all over my mother, like a dismal failure. Worse, I even felt like my father, as if I was some kind of furious beast, torturing my son with tantrums and two-faced philosophies. I had become the persona I had most vigorously striven to avoid.

Back at home the beginning of the following week, and the morning before summer day camp, I told Sam that I didn't want to be friends anymore. I would take care of him as usual because of my fatherly responsibilities, but bike-riding, walking, going to book stores, playing with the computer, all of the things we did together, we would never have to do again; I would never ask him or suggest any of it anymore. I would be his father, for sure, and always love him, but we were finished as pals. I went on and on. I fell completely apart. None of my old standby platitudes made any sense or any impact whatsoever. I felt flummoxed, completely devoid of the muscle of my character. The sound of my voice and the emptiness of my words were humiliating. But I couldn't stop.

As I ranted and raved that morning, I realized how unnerved I had become after our low-clearance encounter in the Atlantic City Holiday Inn, and how important those stories had become in my conception of myself as a father. As I whined and complained, I looked over at Sam in the car seat beside me—his face frozen, his eyes straight ahead, pretending that nothing unusual was happening and that his father was not flipping out in front of his very eyes. This is the way in which Sam deals with serious stress—with an implacable façade, as when he first learned of our divorce. Patricia broke the news one Sunday afternoon in our bedroom. She was lying in the big bed with Sam, the same bed in which she had announced her intentions to me—the bed that she had declared off-limits to any future intimacy—and I was sitting in a chair across the room, trying not to reveal how hard I was trembling. After Patricia explained the situation, the reasons for leaving, and our new living arrangements for Sam—two bedrooms, two houses, next-door neighbors—Sam was silent for a very long time.

"Sam, aren't you going to say anything?" Patricia said. "Do you understand what I've told you? What are you thinking?"

Sam turned to look at us both for the first time. He wasn't smiling, and he wasn't crying. But with his pretty little face and his darting brown eyes, he was somehow able to embrace us simultaneously with his gaze. "As long as we are a family. Even though we don't live together anymore," he added. That was the extent of his response and request—at least up to this moment, a year later. I was certain we would hear more from him about our divorce in the future. But he didn't want to discuss the subject anymore at the time. Now I accepted the fact that he clearly didn't want to discuss bike-riding anymore, either, and so I resolved to act like an adult—a difficult challenge—and move ahead with our relationship, without biking as a male bonding element.

Now, weekdays, I take Sam to school in the mornings, and pick him up after school, play with him, and put him to bed. I take Sam to science camp most every weekend afternoon. We go to Border's Books evenings, browse through the CD section, listen to the free live music and eat our dinners in the cafe. Bedtime reading usually consists of science experiments from the books I buy him, which we discuss with the lights out before he goes to sleep. The following mornings we watch *Cartoon Network*, wrestle, kiss, and tickle—what we like to call "kissaling." After breakfast, we attempt to duplicate experiments we discussed the previous night. We do not ride our bikes, neither Sam nor I, together or individually.

But a couple of months ago, after Patricia bought a bike for commuting to work, Sam announced he was intending to bike-ride with his mother. I changed the subject without a word, barely able to conceal my surprise and feelings of failure. Patricia maintains that she has no intention of riding bikes with Sam—no matter what he might think—until we resolve our bike-riding difficulties. The situation poses an interesting dilemma: Do I wait until Sam decides to reevaluate his riding moratorium with me—no matter how long it takes—and hold Patricia to her promise? Or, do I let Sam bike-ride with his mother, if and when he cares to? Someday he might want to resume our riding excursions—or he might not. This latter option, allowing Sam to go his own way, is the one I will eventually choose simply because I know down deep that it is the only acceptable option, if I intend to be a good role model, even though the sight of Sam and his mother riding together will break my heart. Despite feelings of inadequacy and vulnerability, I realize I will have to trust Sam to do the right thing: to satisfy his own wants and desires and establish acceptable boundaries, while being sensitive and empathetic to the feelings and needs of others, in this case—me.

Inevitably, I will also have to trust myself. I have tried to be a good father and role model and teach Sam to make prudent decisions. If I have done my job, Sam will make the decisions that benefit him the most while hurting other people the least. This is really the collective lesson that the low-clearance stories teach, when you come right down to it—to trust your own instincts despite the consequences; to help people when they are in trouble; to rely on others to help you in times of need and stress. And, most of all, to forgive yourself if you have behaved inappropriately, made the wrong choices, or have suffered defeat or rejection—and move on. To take a deep breath, get up off the ground for the tenth or the eleventh or even the twelfth time, stand up straight, square your shoulders, and drive under another bridge, this time more aware of life's impeccable opportunities—like fatherhood—and the various low-clearance limits that accompany it.

WWMG

One day, about two years into therapy with the psychiatrist I will call Dr. Howard Mason, I was attempting to relate an incident that had occurred when I was thirteen years old, an incident so vivid and frightening that I was unable to remember it all at once. Whenever I started thinking about it—and I found myself reliving snatches once or twice every week—I allowed as much of the memory of that incident to filter back into my mind as I could stand before it became too threatening to endure. I was not haunted by this image, but it was a lingering, unexplored recollection that I could neither eradicate nor confront.

But as I began experiencing the healing that surfaced with the unloading of a lifetime of anxiety on Dr. Mason's shoulders, I noticed that this image was reappearing more frequently, for longer periods, and with sharper resolution of detail. Previously, this memory had returned sporadically and in erratic blurred images, often in black and white. But now I began to visualize swatches of color, blue mostly and yellow—rays from a glaring ball of sun outside a window. The window through which the sun was pouring, I began to see, was in a seventh-grade, junior-high-school classroom. I was sitting in this room at my desk. It was homeroom, where we all reported in the morning for fifteen minutes of school business before heading to our first class.

But there were unusually few students in the room that day. Most of the people missing were boys. This was my first year at Taylor Allderdice, the largest high school in the city, located in a predominantly Jewish community called Squirrel Hill. Coming here from a small elementary school at the far end of the district, most classmates were strangers.

The neighborhood I lived in, Greenfield, was blue collar, working class, friendly, and comfortable, if you were white and Christian, especially Catholic. As I got older, "kike," "dirty Jew" and "Christ killer" were words and phrases I grew accustomed to hearing; I was ambushed and beaten up by neighborhood kids regularly. My parents' promise and my hope at the time I entered Taylor Allderdice was that I would meet kids my age, many of whom were Jewish like me, with whom I could be friends, kids who would not consider me an outsider.

But I soon realized that a shared faith and culture might not be enough to launch new friendships. I didn't fit, didn't dress right, didn't carry myself in the confident way in which these Jewish kids cruised the hallway, greeting one another with a comfortable familiarity that totally eluded me. Listening to their conversations, I learned that they had relationships outside of school, participated in weekend and summer activities different from my own. These kids had no interest in befriending me, a stranger from the wrong side of the district and, in fact, lumped me in with the Greenfield kids I was hoping to escape.

With the exception of the missing students, this particular morning was just like any other. I was sitting at my desk in homeroom waiting for the day to start, watching out the window for the last few stragglers to run across the lush green lawn and up the spacious front steps of the school, when I felt a change in the atmosphere. No noise—just an electric stillness, like that second of a synapse that precedes the thunder and lightning of a violent storm. Then the missing boys began walking into the room, one at a time, grinning sheepishly and self-consciously to one another. Each wore a loose-fitting, crew-neck sweatshirt, gray with blue lettering, displaying four bold initials wwmg.

When I read the words corresponding to the letters—*work-wisdom-morality-goodness*—I realized that it would be impossible for me to be a part of this in-group. It had been totally unrealistic to entertain the possibility of acceptance. These boys, with their long-standing connections from elementary school, religion, or family were now taking steps to define their separateness and close off their circle of intimacy. They had forged a bond, formalized in a fraternity, with a nobility and ethic that I, at thirteen, knew absolutely nothing about. I knew something about work, because I had been sentenced to the prison of my father's shoe store most days after school and on weekends, but the concepts of wisdom, morality, goodness, which these boys had somehow obtained, left me high and dry.

I will never forget my sense of loss and isolation as the boys trooped into the homeroom, the bright rays of the sun streaming through the window, illuminating each of their faces, one after another, like the light from the burning bush on top of Moses' mountain. I found out later that they had planned their dramatic entrance in advance, lining up in the hallway outside the homeroom door to be certain of the class's full attention.

Until now, I had never been able to reconstruct this incident from beginning to end. The exclusion I had experienced was too hurtful, representing a line that was drawn between me and those with whom I had assumed a natural connection. Rejected by the kids and families in Greenfield, I had been assured that ultimate acceptance would occur in Squirrel Hill with the Jews, the Chosen People. But I had been immediately rejected by the chosen few—all of them "my" people—the embodiment of that rejection now contained by those initials and the words behind them: wwmg, *work, wisdom, morality, and goodness*, qualities I had apparently been denied.

Finally able to relive this incident with Dr. Mason in his office, I suddenly realized that many of my life decisions had been shaped by that moment. My drive in high school to become ultra-different, to stop taking my studies seriously, to be rebellious and uncooperative and therefore attract attention to myself, to smoke and drink and become a chronic truant and later to become a hippie, thug motorcyclist, and even later to marry two non-Jewish, nonthreatening women, were all actions in response to these exploding feelings of rejection.

As I sat in Dr. Mason's office and described that incident to him for the second and then a third time, I recalled especially how the sun had spotlighted each boy as he had walked one after another into the room. Suddenly, a familiar face was illuminated in that spotlight, which I instantly freeze-framed. Here was the face of a chubby, curly haired boy I only vaguely remembered, someone with whom I had never spoken, even though we were in the same graduating class and I had seen him and probably indirectly interacted with him at least once or twice each week throughout high school from seventh to twelfth grade. Although time had slimmed his face of baby fat and his name was inexplicably different, I suddenly realized that I knew the man this boy had become. I *trusted* this man; I had confessed, revealed, more of my true, honest, inner self to this man than to anyone else in my entire life.

"You were there," I said, pointing across the shadowed tasteful room at Dr. Howard Mason. "You were one of them! WWMG! Work. Wisdom. Morality. Goodness. You motherfucker," I said to Mason. "You ruined my life."

During two of the nine years I was regularly seeing Dr. Mason, I researched and wrote a book, which documented a season with a crew of National League Baseball umpires. When *The Best Seat in Baseball, But You Have to Stand!* was published the umpires were furious and went to great lengths to insist that what I had written about their feelings concerning the players (whom they resented) and their antics off the field (drinking, partying, and so on) were untrue. They presented a long list of denials concerning the situations I documented, which, they maintained, had never occurred. One of the umpires, Harry Wendelstedt, signed an affidavit attesting to the fact that I had not traveled with his crew, even though two of the umpires signed a similar statement saying that I had been with them through the season.

During the year I had researched the book, I attended the majority of the games that the crew about which I wrote (Doug Harvey, Art Williams, Nick Colosi, and Wendelstedt) officiated. Because of the nonfraternization rules the umpires practiced, I had little to do with the players; I literally immersed myself in the umpire's narrow world. The umpires avoided the media-generated limelight in the cities they visited, staying in smaller hotels and dining at restaurants players normally did not frequent.

I had access to the umpires' locker room in most ballparks. We often traveled together. Their candor about the game, the players, and the pressures under which they worked was enlightening. In our many conversations, they insisted—repeatedly—that somebody (me!) had to capture the drama of the major league umpire experience for the world to witness and therefore understand.

These were passionate and engaging men, mostly, with a sincere reverence for a game in which they were always right—even when they were dead wrong. But this is also what bothered me about the umpires: their inability to accept the limitations of their situation. The men I spent time with—Wendelstedt and Harvey especially—rejected any form of criticism. They refused to contemplate the notion that the very nature of their position attracted resentment and disagreement. "Don't ever let them call you horseshit," is how Doug Harvey explained an umpire's instant obligatory reaction to players, coaches, and managers who questioned their authority and judgment.

The umpires were so convinced of their own righteousness that their jokes and barbs concerning ethnicity and race (Art Williams was the first African American umpire in the National League) were supposed to be presumed harmless just because *they* were saying it. Anyone else joking that they wanted to take a black man fishing, as did Nick Colosi, because "I like to use shiners for bait" would be thrown out of the game and banned from baseball, but not the men in blue. As major league umpires, they could not possibly mean any harm.

Racism emerged as an overriding issue in my book. Pressured by public opinion and the fact that the American League had had an African American umpire for two previous years, Art Williams, a former pitcher for the Detroit Tigers in his middle thirties, was rushed into the position of breaking the racial barrier in the National League with only two years' experience umpiring in the minors. Williams was placed with Wendelstedt and crew chief Doug Harvey, who, before retiring in 1992, became the chief umpire in the league. The fourth crewmember, Nick Colosi, was a waiter at the Copacabana Nightclub in Manhattan during the off-season.

I never had any intention of making this a book about race. I just tried to capture as vividly as possible what took place, what I saw and heard during the season I followed these men around. The hiring of Williams produced tension for a number of reasons— for Williams, who had to prove himself without a lot of umpiring experience and for the three white men who had labored in the minor leagues for many years before ascending to the majors. Most umpires resented Williams's rapid climb, leapfrogging men who had put in their time and paid their dues and were, perhaps, superior umpires. In a macho attempt to deal with the tension, while demonstrating the equality and vulnerability of everyone involved, the umpires' ill-conceived philosophy was to exaggerate the racial schism and stereotype by becoming aggressive and abusive in relation to race and ethnicity, making constant joking references to Williams's skin color, hair and African (i.e., tribal, primitive) background. The balancing factor was to be that Harvey, a Native American, referred to himself as a "dumb Indian," Wendelstedt, a German, said he was a kraut-Nazi, and Colosi called himself the greasy Italian.

The obliviousness and insensitivity that baseball generally and the umpires specifically display toward minorities was reflected when I telephoned the Philadelphia headquarters of what was then the umpires union to ask how many of the sixty-four umpires active in the major leagues were minorities. This took place the year before the umpires' ludicrous power play, in which many of them assumed that major league baseball would be brought to its knees and would give in to many of their demands during a contractual negotiation—if they all resigned.

Ronald Reagan had already demonstrated that few groups in this country are irreplaceable when he refused to cave in to the demands of the air traffic controllers in the early 1980s, who had also threatened to resign en masse if the government did not accept their demands. And the air traffic controllers were doing crucial work—and doing it well under exceedingly difficult circumstances—while the umpires were underqualified and overpaid. They made twice what the air traffic controllers earned.

The umpires' union's expectations had been unrealistic. First, half of the umpires were smart enough to realize that you don't voluntarily walk away from a six-figure income and first-class benefits, including a three-month vacation, over minor workplace issues. They didn't resign. Those who did resign, obviously, were those whose overinflated egos allowed them to believe that they were more important than the game itself. Now, three years later, some of these men are mired in litigation with major league baseball to get their jobs back.

So it isn't surprising, considering their obliviousness to the realities of the world that my question about minorities took a secretary by surprise. She apologetically kept me on hold as she consulted with a number of people. First she got back on the line to report that there were four black umpires, Kerwin Danley, Eric Gregg, Charlie Williams (NL), Chuck Merriweather (AL), and two Latinos, Angel Hernandez (NL) and Richie Garcia (AL). But then she hesitated when someone interrupted her in the background and again put me on hold to consult with someone else. "Five," she said, coming back on the line. "We have five black umpires." She was about to tell me the name of the fifth black umpire in the major leagues when she was once again interrupted and I was again put on hold. "Four," she said, back on the line. "Sorry."

"You don't know how many black umpires you have in the union?" I asked.

"Well," she explained, "one gentlemen once had an Afro, and so we always assumed he was black. But then he cut it off, so now we don't know if he's black or white."

There was some—not a lot—negative publicity around the publication of my book—nothing compared to Jim Bouton's devastating portrait of the major leagues, *Ball Four*. But most of the people I had dealt with in baseball felt betrayed. Soon after the book was published, Fred Fleig, the courtly old gentleman from the National

League who had originally granted me access to the umpires, telephoned and invited me to lunch. We met at a counter in a coffee shop in the Hilton Hotel in Pittsburgh, where Fleig toyed with a bowl of soup and a tuna fish sandwich, continually shaking his head and asking me the same question repeatedly: "Why did you do it? Why did you write what you wrote?"

I had been mostly silent for the forty-five minutes we were together that afternoon. What else could I say, except that I wrote it because it happened.

"But the umpires trusted you," Fleig said, as if that was the reason to have kept my mouth shut.

This issue of trust is one where the professional lives of writers who do what I do, "immersion journalism" or "creative nonfiction," and psychiatrists intersect. "Immersion journalism" can be described, essentially, as the process of hanging around with people about whom you are writing for long periods of time, immersing yourself in their lives and getting to know them on an intimate basis. In addition to the umpires, I've done immersion books with pediatricians, veterinarians, and organ transplant surgeons. In all these situations I have devoted a great deal of time to the lives of the characters I want to write about, listening to them talk, complain, dream, and, in the process, learning their most intimate thoughts and feelings. *Stuck in Time*, in which my friend Daniel was a main character, was about children with severe mental health problems, their parents, and the psychiatrists who treated them. For a long sequence in this book, I arranged to go into therapy with the parents of an adolescent girl suffering from what was thought to be manic depression. The book is written in scenes, just as all creative nonfiction is structured—with dialogue, action, and a taut story—all true.

I first met the Scanlons at the psychiatric facility where I was doing most of my research. I had asked a social worker to connect me to a family that had a successful outcome from the intense treatment offered there. Meggan's behavior had been uncontrollable for years, and no one had ever been able to diagnose her problem—until now. Meggan, at fifteen, had been given lithium, and her behavior immediately became stabilized. After about three months, the triumphant doctors said that it was time for Meggan to be discharged and recommended the family select a private-practice therapist to monitor Meggan's medications and keep their discussions going. Mrs. Scanlon asked a number of friends from her support group and physicians in the hospital for names of the best private-practice therapists. Dr. Kenneth Stanko was the overwhelming choice, but from the moment they first gathered in Stanko's office, it was clear he was the wrong choice and that the dramatic recovery had only been a temporary reprieve.

Sitting in the corner and taking notes from their first weekly meeting to the last, a period of about five months, I observed and documented the tragic collapse of the Scanlon family's temporarily resurrected relationship. In between sessions, I interviewed each family member about their responses to Dr. Stanko's work and I interviewed Dr. Stanko about his objectives, plan of action, and general assessment of what had happened. Dr. Stanko was a solid private-practice therapist who was, unfortunately, unaccustomed to treating such high-maintenance people expecting the on-the-spot attention accorded patients and families in a hospital setting. When he assured the Scanlons that they could call him at home if their disputes escalated uncontrollably, he was being perfectly sincere. But he meant once every three or four weeks—not two or three times a night. One thing that helped Stanko control his resultant irritation and facilitate a switch into a "work mind-set" was money. He billed patients for time on the telephone. Money assuaged his annoyance.

Money was the one and only way in which I had been able to assume a position of influence and power in my dealings with my own psychiatrist. After I first discovered his true identity as a WWMG boy, I did not pay Dr. Mason for his services for nearly two years. What was worse, I pocketed the funds reimbursed to me by the insurance carrier for part of that time and purposely kept myself in arrears for the balance I owed him (20 percent of the total) for almost five years. I know that Dr. Mason was angry, but to his credit, he reminded me only subtly and discreetly from time to time of my debt. Payment is one of the most perplexing problems of practice that therapists face, especially in such a personal and competitive field. Stanko told me that he would often sit with patients, wondering if he should bring up the subject of billing, but he didn't want to give the wrong impression. "They might think: 'Gee, all he is thinking about is getting paid. He's not that interested in us,' " Stanko said.

For her book *Psychoanalysis: The Impossible Profession*, Janet Malcolm conducted interviews with an analyst, Aaron Green, who tells Malcolm of a dinner with friends, nonpsychiatrists, one evening in which they began discussing psychiatrists' fees. "When they started making jokes, I . . . tried very earnestly and seriously to explain how important these things are." But his friends continued to joke until "I lashed out with the most boorish, pontificating, morally outraged tirade—embarrassing everyone there, and most of all me. There I was, an analyst—mature, reflective, well-analyzed (more or less)—acting just like a person. Worse." One of Green's patients whom he saw daily did not pay for eight months. But Green continued the therapy as a symbol of trust—and in hopes that his trust would be rewarded with hard cash. "I consider it one of the most heroic things I have done as an analyst," he said. One day the patient appeared with a check for the entire amount, but then, a few months later, mysteriously stopped paying again.

When I read this passage in Malcolm's book, I immediately juxtaposed Dr. Mason in this situation, discussing me and the fact that I kept him waiting for two years before I was willing to come up with any money. To learn about how he used the money his patients gave him, I looked Mason up in the phone book and, when I discovered he was unlisted, I waited outside of his office one late afternoon and followed him home. He lived on a very fashionable street and in a large and comfortable house in a posh corner of Squirrel Hill, probably not too far from where he grew up in his WWMG world. Following him home, and seeing where he lived, left me somewhat conflicted. My mind rambled. I knew that some of the money he was getting to pay for this residence, a place I could never afford, was coming from me. Not just from my pocketbook or checking account or insurance carrier, but from my gut. I resented such blood money. It was an emotional rape, I concluded, a moral and ethical travesty that he was able to sit and listen (or pretend to listen) to my innermost thoughts and get paid so handsomely.

But, of course, my problems were more difficult and complicated than the average run-of-the-mill patient. It was okay for the Scanlons to have selected an ordinary human being for a shrink in Dr. Stanko. My case required extraordinary skill and sensitivity. I had been emasculated and misunderstood. Only a special person could fathom what I had been through as a child—a manipulating mother, an abusive father, an isolating environment—could listen so carefully and with such intensity that they could pinpoint the subtle secrets embedded in my ramblings and delicately help me isolate and probe those very tender heretofore camouflaged life-shaping experiences. If my shrink lived in modest surroundings and charged affordable rates, it would have devalued him and his potential to help me. I would have lost faith.

After all, it was Mason who helped coax forth the image-defining, image-destroying WWMG incident of my life. "Coax forth" was the right term to use. He helped mine my inner psyche by subtle actions, not words—a philosophy and technique that significantly impacted my own immersion nonfiction research work. I consider being shrunk by Dr. Mason a writing apprenticeship. Had I not been shrunk by Mason, I would never have coaxed forth the umpires' natural behavior or Stanko's angst; I know that my subjects would have always doubted me.

I learned from Mason that communication begins with listening. Stanko was candid not because I was charismatic or asked probing questions but because of the way in which I listened to him. I never took my eyes off him while he was talking. Even during note taking, I nodded, and I always responded with appropriate body language (a wrinkled brow, a chagrined expression, and so on) for every twist and turn in his story. This was how I collected information from all of the people about whom I have written over the years. It is not the art of writing per se, or even the skill in planning the questions you intend to ask that count the most, but the intensity with which you listen that paves the way for the best story to be told. I think I knew this when I first began hanging out with the umpires, but my interactions with Mason helped me to understand the similarities between our professions and the ways in which writers could learn from therapists: that everyone has stories to tell, including and especially therapists, and that they will tell those stories to any person willing to make a sincere effort to listen to the "whole" story.

This is where a traditional journalist will go awry, by being so concerned with quotes and sound bites that they don't wait for the real or larger story to surface. The approach practiced by Dr. Mason on me elicited secrets and pent-up resentments that might have remained buried for a lifetime. Being willing to wait as long as it takes—and follow an endless road of twists and turns in the narrative until the real story emerges—is as imperative in psychiatry as it is in writing and reporting. This is what engenders trust: that you, the writer or the therapist, are willing to give your most precious possession, time, as much as it takes, to listen to a subject purge, discover, reveal, and reinvent himself. Although writers and psychiatrists have different goals, they will often push the same emotional buttons, triggering dramatic and deep-seated responses. In both situations, money is an important reward.

Here is the scenario which took place before almost every session I conducted with Dr. Stanko: I would come into his office and sit in one of his comfortable easy chairs with a table beside it and set up my Radio Shack Micro-26 voice-activated micro-recorder. As I turned it on and propped it upright on the table in full view, Stanko would also say, *he would never fail to say*: "And how do I know that you are going to use the information I am providing in a fair and equitable way?" And I would look at him and raise my eyebrows in an amused but questioning manner, because it was a Q-and-A sequence we had gone through at least a half-dozen times, to which he would respond by waving his hand, palm forward, and smiling somewhat shyly and insecurely, "I know, I know . . . I have to trust you."

Trust was also the watchword in my relationship with Dr. Mason, as it needs to be in any therapeutic setting. I trusted him—I had to trust him with the most intimate secrets of a lifetime. All my life I had felt angry and isolated, alone in a sea of personal subterfuge. I had no friends or confidants. Keeping my feelings to myself may have made me look strong and independent on the outside, but inside I was fearful and angry. I wanted to know why—and I wanted to release the pressure of my anger. I had hated the WWMG boys from the moment they revealed themselves, and I had taken what had happened—being excluded—quite personally, as if Mason and his Squirrel Hill cronies had planned my humiliation. But they had no reason to hurt me; they had no reason to know who I was—or to know if I was inferior. Which is what I eventually realized, as I tried to process the notion that Dr. Mason was one of those despicable WWMG boys who, as a group, precipitated the worst years of my life. Mason may have been guilty of self-centeredness, but not of malice. After all, he had been an adolescent—no more sensitive or mature than I. And it also dawned on me that he, like me, harbored his own secrets to reveal.

"Why did you change your name?" I demanded at our next session. Instantly, his real name had come back to me; I visualized him the way he had been a quarter of a century before. "You were Mendelssohn—not Mason; you were Jewish, like all of the rest of those bastards in Squirrel Hill who rejected me."

For the first time in our relationship, Mason was visibly upset and uncontrolled. His usually passive pale face flushed with humiliation. "It is a long story, and I don't want to get into it," he said. "Changing my name seemed like the right thing to do at the time . . . I'm not sure if I should have done it, but you never know how things are going to turn out," he added.

Then he lapsed into an awkward silence, and we stared at each other, listening to the clock beside his table click-clicking up until the time for talk was over and I silently jumped to my feet, walked out of the office and out onto the street without saying goodbye.

As to whether he really had recognized me all along and had been waiting for this moment of discovery and revelation—or dreading it—I should say that, although it was a very likely possibility, I decided that it didn't matter. I had made my decision to trust someone—a decision that had to do with how much you trust yourself and the people with whom you share intimacies. For whatever reason, I had instinctively put my faith in Dr. Mason/Mendelssohn, who had devoted his time listening to me, and I was not willing to pack my bags and go elsewhere after investing so much of my true innermost self and receiving so much insight in return, even though all the insight gained was mine.

This is what happens in immersion journalism or creative nonfiction—the product of what I do. By listening to the people about whom I am writing, by being the most hardworking and earnest listener possible, people like the Scanlons and Dr. Stanko confide in me. I nod at their insight, smile at their jokes, grimace at their misery and always give good eye contact, while revealing as little as possible of myself, except when that revelation validates my subject's own feelings and ideas or leads to information I have been wanting to know. I will usually not ask questions; rather, I nudge the conversation in a direction that suits my needs and wait for the information to surface.

I was not angry with Dr. Mason. How could I be angry when Dr. Mason, whatever his lapses, helped me unearth a painful, haunting memory. The WWMG story opened the innermost doors to my life, shedding light on who I was—and why I conducted myself the way I did. I trusted Mason, my psychiatrist, and the Scanlon family and Dr. Stanko had trusted me, their earnest and faithful listener. Mrs. Scanlon had revealed her desperate, innermost thoughts—and invited me to be a silent listener in their intimate family therapy sessions. At one point she announced that her life was so horrible that she was going to kill herself—and she invited her husband and teenage son to destroy themselves with her.

Before sending the book to my publisher, I telephoned Elizabeth and Tom Scanlon and explained to them that the portrait I painted of their family did not look particularly favorable. I asked them if they wanted to read what I had written before the draft was submitted. As much as they have poured out their hearts and insisted that people must know their stories, my subjects will invariably have serious reservations when they see their stories through the eyes of an observer and begin to realize that they are opening themselves up for the world to see. The Scanlons took the manuscript for the weekend and promised to call me Monday morning. I waited throughout the day—Monday, Tuesday, and then Wednesday, fearing that the Scanlons had read what I had written and had immediately, upon their return, contacted their attorney to stop publication of the book. Feeling desperate on Thursday morning, I telephoned Elizabeth at home, but she did not return my call until the following afternoon.

"The first time we read the book, we were very angry," she told me, "and so we read it a second and third time, and we were still angry. But the more we discussed the book, the more we realized that we were angry at ourselves and at the world for having played such a terrible trick on us. We have a mentally ill, out-of-control daughter, and we are helpless to do anything about it. Every day we fight to survive, which is the story you have told. It isn't a pretty story, but we trusted you, and you told the truth." But the umpires had also trusted me—and I had also told the truth; but they were furious with me. I don't think I can pinpoint what I did wrong. Either I told too much of the truth—or not enough. The truth in itself is not the goal all parties are seeking or endorsing; rather, it is their own conception of the truth they condone. Dr. Stanko hasn't been in contact with me since the book was written, but the Scanlons and I have remained friends because our understanding of the truth coincided.

Coincidentally, Dr. Stanko's office was in the same building as was Dr. Mason's, and positioned in the same room, just one floor below. In the five months that I rendezvoused with the Scanlons and Stanko in that building, I never once saw Dr. Mason. By this time, I had been free of therapy and out of contact with Dr. Mason for at least a decade. But when I sat in that easy chair, smiled at Dr. Stanko, revealed my tape recorder, and waited for Stanko to say what he would never fail to say, I always experienced the overwhelming feeling that I had accomplished what most veteran subjects of psychotherapy secretly wish for: I was, at those moments, in that chair, in the same room and building, one floor below, transposing myself into a different time warp and to another level of consciousness and awareness. I was, in my mind, shrinking my shrink.

Once I mustered up the courage to broach the subject of ending therapy—leaving Dr. Mason—it turned out to be a relatively simple and comparatively painless process.

I told Mason that I thought it was time to get back into a life on my own without his overwhelming presence. He replied in his ever-so-calm-and-collected fashion that it sounded like a good idea, and we established a date a couple of weeks in the future when the break-off would occur. When our final session was over, I walked out the door, elevatored to the lobby, and ambled out into the sunlight. I had thought for certain that I would be an emotional wreck, but I felt only mildly shaken. This was an underwhelming conclusion to a nine-year ordeal, I thought, as I walked toward my car. And then I had a vision. I am not prone to having such mystical experiences, but this was startling.

Suddenly, looming in front of me, was an image of a little girl. It was Patricia, my wife: how she looked in a photo when she was in the second grade, which she had once given me during that period of intense infatuation between us when it was okay for her to be "my little girl." At that moment, I suddenly knew what I had to have happen in my life next and what I had been doing over the past nine years with Dr. Mason, vetting my awful memories. I had been preparing myself for fatherhood. I was ready finally to be an adult, to be responsible for a child, to become a father, to have a family. I was no longer afraid of commitment or entanglement or of ruining my life and someone else's life through uncontrollable bursts of anger any longer. My own father's legacy—his bad seed—was no longer my fate.

The fact that I wanted to be a father was too much for Patricia, who feared that a child would jeopardize our relationship. For ten years we had done virtually everything together, to the exclusion of the outside world: aerobics classes, walking vacations, movies. We made few friends and talked primarily with each other, even in the most public venues.

Once a child entered into the picture our lives would change drastically, she said. We battled constantly from that point onward. Evenings, weekends, vacations. It took years to begin intelligent discussions, for she literally stonewalled the subject of children and family—would explode in a tirade of denial whenever I brought it up. But the fact that I realized I wanted to become a father was the most important thing that ever happened to me. It was more an expression of my own self and confidence than anything else I have ever done in my life—because my own father figure had been so disappointing and hurtful. It was for these same reasons that Patricia was terrified of becoming a mother.

It is ironic to look back at those years of turmoil and debate with Patricia—and wrenching change. Much of what Patricia feared most—the loss of her career that had taken her so long to achieve, the dissolution of our relationship—eventually came true, but at her own instigation. The fact that she became a terrific and dedicated mother, instantly, overnight, changed her life—as fatherhood changed mine. In the process, it destroyed our marriage.

Dr. Mason has come into my life on two occasions since I stopped therapy fifteen years ago. The first time was the morning after Patricia announced her intention of divorcing me.

That morning, I realized that facing my computer and attempting to continue working on my current book project would not be practical or productive so I decided to go to the nearby Starbucks. I would bring my notebook and attempt to jump-start my work there. I could then continue my writing back at my home office later in the morning after I had taken Sam to school and my wife left the house to go to work. I dressed hurriedly and jumped in the car. I arrived just in time for the 6 A.M. opening and already there was a black Volvo station wagon glinting in the yellow-beamed spotlights of the parking lot. Inside, there was a lone figure hunched over a newspaper at the opposite end of the shop, evidently the owner of the Volvo.

After a while, he got up and walked over to the serving counter and asked for a refill; I could see his reflection in the glass of the front window through which I was peering, but I needn't have looked. I recognized his voice. My heart smashed against the inside wall of my chest, as I was struck by the incredible and undeniable meaning of the coincidence. After fifteen years of silence, Dr. Howard Mason, in some ways a virtual stranger and in other ways the single most important figure of my life, had suddenly reappeared—and at a time I needed him the most. I turned to attract his attention. He came toward me, extending his hand. "I thought I recognized you when you came in," he said.

"Is this your morning hangout?" I said.

"Two or three times a week," he replied. "How are you doing?" he asked me, softly, with his best seductive intonation. As I paused to allow the sound of his voice and the intensive and intimate warmth of his manner to gush back into me and engulf me with infantile feelings of safety and escape from danger, I realized that this was my moment of reckoning. Dr. Mason had helped me through my last divorce, and now he had magically appeared to help me through my second marital disaster. But after that initial rush of relief and escape, I realized that I didn't need him. His sudden and coincidental appearance there at Starbucks the morning after the disaster of my marriage, actually enhanced my trust of myself. It reminded me of what I had learned—my strength and my inner capacity to deal with the most challenging and trying of circumstances. This is what therapists are supposed to do for their patients, I think—prepare them to be emotionally independent, to not panic when experiencing the familiar and frightening rush of anxiety, to, essentially, learn to "shrink" themselves.

One time when our sessions had been especially intense, and when I began having second thoughts about being able to manage without his help and without regular therapy, he had told me that wherever I was I would be able to hear his voice at times of indecision and crisis. He did not mean that I would actually hear him advising me about what to do, but that I would be able to remember how I had responded in similar difficult situations and, more than that, I would recall that, by acting instinctively and logically, I had survived every major crisis in my life. I had been hurt, but had always been able to rebound in a way that made me proud of myself and had enhanced the shape of my character. I must know and accept the probability, he told me, that I would have more hard times in my life, that I would experience anxiety and depression, but I must learn to trust myself and, just as importantly, trust that if ever I really did need him, he—Dr. Howard Mason—would be available. I don't believe that our coincidental connection at Starbucks was some sort of mystical sign that the great spirits were beaming Mason's energy down toward me, but I felt exceedingly fortunate that it had happened; his presence demonstrated my strength and independence.

"I'm fine, Dr. Mason," I told him, after pausing for a while. "Never better."

The next time I saw Dr. Mason I was on the Nordic Track at the health club I belong to, and he was sitting directly to my left on an Ergometer rowing machine, huffing and puffing and red-faced from effort. I climbed off the Track, walked over, shook his hand and welcomed him to the club; I am a longtime member, and he informed me that he had just joined a few months before.

"So after all of these years we finally belong to the same club," I said.

"What do you mean?" he said.

"Remember WWMG?" I reminded him.

But instead of smiling and nodding or rolling his eyes or responding in an otherwise knowing manner, Dr. Mason looked at me blankly. Clearly, he didn't know what I was talking about. Had he forgotten the connection—*my connection, our connection* to another club, WWMG? I looked at him intensely, searching his eyes for awareness or acknowledgment. I won't say that I was unaffected by the fact that my psychiatrist of nine gut-wrenching years couldn't recall the single most influential incident of my life and his active involvement in it. I was humbled. But the fact that he didn't remember made me feel more ordinary and thereby more healthy. It may have loomed as a large incident in my life—it was—but in the overall scheme of things, my WWMG encounter and the scars it had precipitated were, in psychiatric parlance, "unremarkable." I was one of perhaps a thousand patients Dr. Howard Mason had tended to, and I had naively assumed that he would remember the most salient details about me. I suppose a psychiatrist's patients have a way of inflating their own importance. So do students, as I had realized when I cornered Mr. Meyers on a downtown Pittsburgh street not many years before.

"We Want More Girls," Mason then said, looking up from the Ergometer, smiling.

"Pardon me? What did you say?" I leaned forward to hear him more clearly. There were dark pockets of sweat under his T-shirt. I recognized the faint and familiar aroma of the deodorant that club management provided members in the bathrooms.

"We Want More Girls," he repeated, rowing back and forth. "That's what WWMG means."

"That's not want it means," I replied impatiently. "There were those other words . . ."

Dr. Mason laughed, but I did not laugh with him. "You mean 'Work-Wisdom-Goodness-Morality'?"

"That's right," I said, "the real words."

He shook his head, as he continued to stroke. The sound of the sliding track and the rhythmic timing of his stroke suddenly reminded me of masturbation. Was I being mastered, manipulated, or masturbated once again by my shrink? Or was this payback on behalf of his brother-in-therapy, Kenneth Stanko?

"When we started the club, the real words we came up with were 'We Want More Girls.' But we knew the school would not authorize a club called 'We Want More Girls' and our parents would forbid us to join such a club even if it were authorized. So we kept the initials and made up a respectable name."

"So that's how you came to WWMG?" I asked. "It had nothing to do with . . ."

"Work, wisdom, morality, and goodness?" he interrupted. "No way."

"Why didn't you tell me this before?"

He looked at me quizzically. It wasn't clear if he realized why he should have been providing me with this information—or when—but it really didn't matter. "Everybody knew," he pointed out. What he meant was that everybody who mattered, everyone who was in some way "connected" to or affiliated with the "anointed" group—the chosen few—knew.

I nodded at Dr. Mason, said goodbye, and returned to the Nordic Track. I put the plastic rope handles in my hands and fitted my feet into the rubber stirrups, but then I couldn't move. I stared at Mason's back as he continued stroking. Here I stood after nine years of therapy, two marriages, a virtual operetta of insecurities about my character and masculinity and body image and what do I finally learn? That work, wisdom, morality, and goodness had nothing to do with what made the boys of whom I was so jealous consider themselves so superior. That, in fact, there was no real reason for the aura of superiority that had engulfed the room when the WWMG boys made their dramatic entrance. It was a state of mind—ungrounded in reality. They were nothing special. These boys were driven by the same basic instincts that have obsessed me through a lifetime—more girls, more sex, more recognition, more money.

After all this time, could that possibly be true? "Of course," I said, aloud, as I stood there balanced but not yet moving on the Nordic Track. Even though it was obviously true and had always been obviously true, this was suddenly a great revelation to me. "Of course," I said again. "Of course."

I had always known that, biologically, we non-WWMG boys were the same as WWMG members: substance and matter, blood and muscle and bone. Undoubtedly, we were also alike intellectually and psychologically. Then what led them to believe that they were better than I was—better than almost anybody? Perhaps because they feared that they weren't better and that the combined power of their numbers provided them with a hollow confidence they could not achieve standing alone? Why had I assumed I was not as good as they were?

And what of Dr. Mason's intentions and his overall recollections? Should he have enlightened me about the WWMG acronym at that integral moment of my therapy when I had realized that he had been a member of this group that had been so devastating to me? Or had he, in fact, enlightened me? Perhaps he told me everything in one of our sessions, spilled the beans, while I listened and nodded— and refused to process the truth. But I might have not wanted to hear the truth at the moment. My anger, after all, energized and sustained me. I had been driven by the wrongs I had intended to right, by the conviction that I was the classic, misunderstood underdog, forced to crawl my way to the top against seemingly insurmountable odds.

Or had he assumed that I knew because everybody else knew the real words behind the WWMG smoke screen? Or did he actively make the decision to not enlighten me because, as a shrink, he was charged with the task of listening to desperate people and encouraging their innermost explorations—and not providing answers and explanations?

I have pondered these questions since that incident at the Ergometer occurred. Conceivably, Mason told me the meaning of WWMG when I was his patient—it was certainly no big secret, at least as he recalls it now. But more than likely, whether or not he told me, I lacked the psychological capability to embrace the notion—to accept the raw and confounding truth. In my life, I have gone far—driven to achieve something significant by the blinding, impenetrable barrier of alienation with which I was confronted at home and in school. Maybe I did not want to learn that my battles, my resentments, had been unnecessary, had fueled fires that did not have to burn.

These are the questions and answers I have pondered since I returned to the Nordic Track, retreating from Dr. Mason's revelation, resuming my workout in the same dogged manner as I had resumed my life after the WWMG incident, after the military and my temporary escape from Pittsburgh and my change in body image climaxed by the rope test, my discovery of books and writing which, combined, had been my salvation. And here are my conclusions, as of this moment, years of contemplation later. I can't guarantee that my conclusions won't change as I continue to gather more information about my life, which will inevitably occur as I get older and as everyone else around me gets younger and it becomes much easier to look back in time and not forward.

So: while it may well be true that there were always two WWMG meanings, I am relatively certain that Work, Wisdom, Morality, and Goodness was everyone's first choice and belief. I will never forget the way those boys marched into our homeroom classroom on that day so many years ago. They were so beamingly full of themselves as members of their elite group, so aware of the glue that bound them, the glue of their sweatshirts, their destiny, and the process of exclusion that led them to this triumphant moment in their short but irrefutably superior lives.

There was no snickering or winking at their secret. This promenade was not a joke, had nothing to do with girls, sex, dating, or lust. It was a definitive statement not of what they wanted, but of who they were and what they were destined to become which, whatever it was, would turn out better than anyone else not associated with WWMG—or so they thought. There were few boys growing up in the late 1950s and early 1960s in middle America at the ages of eleven or twelve who cared one hoot about girls, especially in comparison to how much they cared about how they were perceived by other boys. The culture and depth of sexual awareness were different for preadolescent boys then. Later, as the boys of WWMG matured, girls became a driving force. Then an obvious and subtle switch occurred from Work, Wisdom, Morality, and Goodness to a more plausible and highly humorous We Want More Girls. Dr. Mason may choose to believe, may find comfort in believing, that his order of events, his definition of reality, is correct. But his perspective is flawed because he was part of the group that precipitated the alienation—and not one of the victims, like me.

Which is not to say that my perspective isn't also flawed to an extent. I was, after all, not part of the in-group, not one of the marchers, so I couldn't really know or understand the pressures that were being exerted upon them and the standards to which they were forcing themselves to live up to. These were the boys of whom their parents and communities expected great things; they were to be the political leaders, the rabbis, the dentists, the financiers, who would assume key positions in synagogue and city, the *psychiatrists*, even, who would skillfully safeguard Squirrel Hill psyches. What if they had failed, lost their luster and buoyancy? What if, God forbid, they slipped down into the briny sea where we common and flawed folk—the masses—were settled, experiencing life from the bottom, as foot soldiers, rather than at the top, in the cavalry, as officers, on a high horse, fulfilling the WWMG legacy?

Maybe I am being too hard on them and on Dr. Mason—unfair. After all, he changed my life, helped me through a period of torturous traumatic stress. But Dr. Mason is the only WWMG person with whom I ever connected—the symbol of the event in my life that most flummoxed me. I will never forget WWMG. The scars inflicted upon a person's psyche are indelible. Scars from your psychiatrist, scars from your peers, scars from your teachers and rabbis, scars from your parents, scars inflicted upon oneself. None of them go away. But you try to reach a point in your life when you can see the scars every day, and when the sight of them makes you smarter by reminding you of what you have learned and can continue to learn from the pain they represent. But usually they don't hurt anymore—except sometimes when it rains, as when people in whom you have confidence and trust turn against you, disappoint you, as I disappointed the umpires and Dr. Stanko, and as Dr. Mason and my classmates and my two ex-wives, my former beloveds, disappointed me.

That's my reality, at least at the moment. I won't forget, but I will forgive, and I will move forward into yet another phase of my life a little less handicapped than in the phase before. This is the lesson I take from my first fifty-plus years: to forgive and not forget and, hopefully, to be forgiven my mistakes but not forgotten for my kindnesses, my quirks, my contributions and accomplishments, however insignificant. And, most important, to trust: If I hadn't trusted Dr. Mason, hadn't been able to look beyond the hurt he had inflicted on me as a WWMG, I would not have been able to write this story, to have become a father of Sam and even a Godfather. But trusting other people is the easy part. With Dr. Mason's help, I learned to listen to my instincts, to look at people with a three-dimensional perspective and to trust myself, which, in the end, is the opening gateway beyond which the trust of other people occurs, and thus, an impeccable accomplishment of a lifetime.

Intimate Details

I was returning to Pittsburgh through New York's LaGuardia Airport—my first visit since the September 11 terrorist attacks. The security guard, a short, slender Latino in his late twenties, quickly rifled through my clothes and papers, but it was my shaving kit that attracted most of his attention. I had arrived an hour and a half before my scheduled flight, hoping to go standby on an earlier flight leaving in twenty-five minutes. So I was conscious of the seconds ticking away.

This man was intense and meticulous. He opened the top of my water-resistant, metallic-blue Mini Mag-Lite and examined the batteries—an emergency item I now carry wherever I go, in response to being trapped in the Georgetown Inn during that twenty-six-hour blackout and almost killing myself in the pitch black trying to locate and navigate the emergency exit. But the guard found a second flashlight, a white plastic rectangular miniature from the Western Pennsylvania Cardiovascular Institute—a place I'd never heard of. The batteries were corroded and had leaked onto the case, so I threw it away. I don't know how it got there.

He also discovered two nail clippers with miniature nail files about an inch long with moderately sharp points. If I intended to keep the nail files, he would have to check my shaving kit, tag it, and send it separately as baggage, he said. I suggested he break them off from the clippers and discard them. We also trashed the cuticle scissors I use to trim my mustache.

Next he unscrewed the top from my After Bite Itch Eraser, housed in a plastic tube the size of a ballpoint pen. It had a metal clip to attach to a shirt pocket. He touched the tip of his finger to the roller-ball applicator and glanced up at me suspiciously. I turned away. No event in my past precipitated After Itch, but I like being prepared for the unexpected. It enhances my trust in myself.

The guard opened my cinnamon-flavored Blistex, my Advanced Formula Krazy Glue, my waxed CVS Dental Tape and my septic stick, and he sniffed my prescription-strength Cruex cream (for jock itch). I also had a small bottle of Listerine in the bag, an Arrid XX Ultra Clear Anti-Perspirant & Deodorant Solid and one NaturaLamb condom. He did not open the Tic Tac box in which I store my emergency medications—aspirin, Motrin, sinus pills, and laxatives—and did not ask me why I had three half-used toothpaste tubes, two travel toothbrushes, two Gillette Mach 3 razors and one Schick disposable razor. I couldn't have answered. I just put things in this kit spontaneously, whenever it occurs to me that I might need them. Like I said, I always try to be prepared for the unexpected.

This is a very small, black canvas shaving kit by Edge Creek, which manufactures compact equipment for backpackers. It has three parts that fold into a bulky little package about the size of a paperback pocket dictionary. Unfolded, it has a hook to hang on a tree branch (or towel bar), and a tiny mirror to use for shaving. Not that this man cared about the origin of the kit or the reasons for any of its contents. In light of the September 11 catastrophes at the World Trade Center and the Pentagon and in Somerset County, Pennsylvania, he had a suddenly high-profile job to do—a responsibility completely unrelated to revealing anything about my identity, other than the search for contraband that could endanger my fellow passengers or alter in any way the safe completion of my flight.

But I couldn't help feeling, as I stood at the table near the security area with people waiting behind me to have their own bags checked and simultaneously observing what I had in mine, that my life was now an open book and that I had somehow lost a significant measure of my privacy and dignity. I had felt this same way when I was in the military sleeping with eighty men in the same room.

There was nowhere to hide; we were all so exposed to each other. Which had made my private refuge in the base library so crucial. Without the library and the books it offered, I might never have learned to acknowledge and live with my double image.

Of course we have all been faced with a foreboding and growing sense of loss since the horror of September 11, and I don't intend to compare the minor indignity I suffered at LaGuardia to the major devastation of those who lost lives, loved ones, or livelihoods. But every day since September 11, we have discovered ways in which our daily routines and the freedoms we have taken for granted have been substantially altered by those horrific events. Extra security and delays at airports and in public buildings are more than minor annoyances: They are symbols of an increasingly altered and dangerous world.

I was fortunate to know only two people directly affected by this horrible tragedy. Fred is a high-ranking executive in a major international financial institution with a large Wall Street facility. Lynn, his wife, is an artist whose bold canvases electrify their sprawling, high-tech TriBeCa loft. The first plane literally buzzed their loft before crashing into the WTC. Lynn was in the shower and heard the sickening sound of collision. She said to her husband, "Something terrible must have happened down in the street." He went to the window and then shouted for her to come running.

They sat on their living room sofa, screaming and weeping and watching tiny figures—real people—leaping out of windows sixty stories above the street, with American Airlines Flight 11 hanging precariously from the WTC, piercing the heart of the financial district. Friends from neighboring lofts joined them. Together they witnessed the second collision and experienced the paralyzing and petrifying horror of the blitzkrieg. Later, as survivors covered with inches of searing ash fled the devastation, Lynn and Fred rushed into the street and escorted the dazed victims into their apartment so they could wash themselves and call their families. Soon after the buildings collapsed, the water that came from their tap turned brown.

Writing in the *New York Times* nearly three weeks afterward, H. R.

Kleinfeld talked about the aroma of the ash and of the ceaselessly smoldering buildings. "It's the odor of a burning computer. Or a burning tire. Or burning paper," Kleinfeld observed. "One person said it was the scent of unsettled souls." When I visited Ground Zero that week, the aroma continued to pervade the air. It clung to my lungs like a living organism. I can still feel it, a scratching, haunting residue of those innocent victims whose lives were stolen from their children, families, and countries. It is a tragedy and a crime that reverberates far beyond the barricades and the police and National Guard checkpoints that surrounded the crime scene perimeter six months later.

Kleinfeld said, "A few people had their jacket collars pressed against their noses. A few others had tied handkerchiefs around their faces, bandit style. One young man simply pinched his nose with his fingers as he walked. A middle-aged woman had folded an American flag over her mouth."

This searing, sensory grimness was shared—and embraced—daily by a hoard of observers. The day I visited, tourists were pointing and clicking disposable cameras at the smoldering ruins partially concealed by dumpsters and dump trucks. Police and National Guard in camouflage were everywhere, as were the media—notebooks in hand. TV reporters stood on makeshift platforms so the rubble could be seen behind them as they talked. Paralleling the aroma, an all-pervading quiet hung in the air. In contrast to the usual noisy cacophony of New York—a symphony of horns, trucks, traffic, hucksters, cell phones, and people shouting to be heard over every distraction—there was a startling edge of restraint. The boldness that characterizes city life was missing at Ground Zero and virtually everywhere else I visited in the city.

Earlier that day at Café Europa, a favorite midtown morning haunt across from Carnegie Hall, the wait staff was unusually friendly, greeting me as if I were a long-lost friend, though I am certain they hardly remembered me. They presented a free chocolate cookie with my Portobello sandwich. A man in a purple sweater, yellow jacket, and silk scarf sang to the music, smiling warmly over his tuna-salad sandwich. It occurred to me that I had never heard music at Café Europa before, perhaps because the place was usually mobbed at breakfast and lunch. Now, at 11:45 A.M., there were just six patrons. I won't soon forget the scene at Europa, the aroma of which Kleinfeld writes, the water turning brown in Lynn and Fred's loft, or the crusts of ash clinging to the people stumbling from the wreckage—not only because the reality of the experience is so stark, but also because the images are so specific and intimate.

This is a lesson that writers of all genres need to know—that the secret to making prose and poetry memorable and therefore vital and important is to catalog with specificity the details that are most intimate. By *intimate* I mean ideas and images that readers won't easily imagine—ideas and images you observed that symbolize a memorable truth about the characters or the situations that concern you. That's one aspect of intimacy that readers demand.

In the introduction to his breakthrough 1973 anthology, *The New Journalism*, Tom Wolfe writes about how Jimmy Breslin, a columnist for the *New York Herald Tribune*, captured the realistic intimacy of experiences by noticing details that could act as metaphors for something larger and more all-encompassing that he wanted to say. Wolfe describes Breslin's coverage of the trial of Anthony Provenzano, a union boss charged with extortion. At the beginning, Breslin introduces the image of the bright morning sun bursting through the windows of the courtroom and reflecting off the large diamond ring on Provenzano's chubby pinky finger. Later, during a recess, Provenzano, flicking a silver cigarette holder, paces the halls, sparring with a friend who came to support him, the sun still glinting off the pinky ring.

Wolfe writes: "The story went on in that vein with Provenzano's Jersey courtiers circling around him and fawning while the sun explodes off his pinky ring. Inside the courtroom itself, however, Provenzano starts getting his. The judge starts lecturing him and the sweat starts breaking out on Provenzano's upper lip. Then the judge sentences him to seven years, and Provenzano starts twisting his pinky finger with his right hand." The ring is a badge of Provenzano's ill-gotten labors, symbolic of his arrogance and his eventual vulnerability and resounding defeat.

Although we can't achieve such symbolism each time we capture an incident, writers who want their words to be remembered beyond the date on which their stories are published or broadcast will seek to capture the special observations that symbolize the intimacy to which they have been exposed. The details the security guard revealed about me by unpacking my shaving kit in front of a half-dozen strangers were not so shockingly intimate, but they were specific and revealing. You can piece together snatches of who I am and the way I am by thinking about my flashlight, my Itch Eraser, my Cruex, and my triple toothbrushes and razors.

It is true that I am a bit absent-minded and also somewhat cautious. I back myself up with flashlights and salves so as to avoid situations that may annoy me or curtail my activities. If I confessed these traits in an essay, you would not necessarily find them memorable, but now, with the specifics of my shaving kit, a porthole into my personality has been revealed.

The earlier flight I had hoped to make was boarding when I had finally worked my way through security. I rushed to see if I could get on. But I suddenly stopped to consider: It was at a gate that I had never used at LaGuardia for a Pittsburgh flight. I had used this gate to go to Washington DC and Boston, but never Pittsburgh. The flight was open. I could have gotten on and arrived back home to see Sam before he went to bed. If I waited, I might not talk with him until the following morning. But the vibes weren't right. For no reason whatsoever, except for the gnawing feelings of foreboding inside me, I knew I shouldn't take that flight.

So I retreated to the U.S. AIRWAYS Club, nibbled on snack mix, sipped coffee for ninety minutes and stared out the window. My flight departed from Gate 12—the gate I almost always use when flying from LaGuardia to Pittsburgh—and I felt a lot better about traveling. Nothing eventful occurred on the earlier flight (I checked, back in Pittsburgh) but now you know something else about me. I am cautious, but above all else, I continue to listen to my instincts, no matter how illogical they seem. I trust myself.

Why did I go to New York in the first place? Because I felt compelled to get on a plane in order to break the spell of hesitation and alienation cast by September 11. Normally I am on the road for a day nearly every week, but after September 11, I remained in my neighborhood for more than a month. I felt compelled to experience New York, to understand that in almost every respect it was the same city as before—more sober, wounded, and scarred, but inherently unbreakable. And I wanted to prove myself unbreakable. I want my willingness to confront adversity to be a metaphor of my life. By "confront," I don't mean to say, "fight." Confronting adversity can and should mean understanding your strengths and vulnerabilities and learning to work within them—and reach, gradually, beyond them.

Like the city of New York, we must all learn to reach beyond the wounds in our heart to that place where the strength of our character is anchored. I can visualize that spot inside of me: the knots of the rope in boot camp when I finally passed the rope test; the fire in Willard Mixon's eyes, which burned deep into Chief Petty Officer O'Reilly; the words I write in this book, which allow me to come clean with my readers and myself; Rabbi Poupko's fingers pressing into my shoulders; the nauseating frustration of my temper tantrums when I could not be the person I wanted to be for Sam. These images, which once humiliated me, now sustain my resiliency.

Our country in my lifetime has bounced back from many disasters—the assassinations of JFK, MLK, RFK, the protests against the Vietnam War, the continued turmoil of racism, and much more—because we, as a nation, are deeply and solidly anchored. I like to think that I am, too. I have good values and self-respect. I have learned to listen, to imagine, to resurrect painful memory and, through deep reflection, find meaning and direction from the winding, bumpy road of my past.

But isn't that to be expected if you are the Godfather Behind Creative Nonfiction? Who else—but me—can make you an offer you cannot refuse?

Source Acknowledgments

The following essays in this collection have been previously published: Portions of "Who . . . What . . . Is Crazy?" appeared in *Stuck in Time: The Tragedy of Childhood Mental Illness* (New York: Henry Holt, 1993), 1–6, © copyright 1993 by Lee Gutkind, reprinted by arrangement with Henry Holt, and in *God's Helicopter* (Pittsburgh: Slow Loris Press, 1983); "Dog Story" (previously titled "Icy") from *The Veterinarian's Touch: Profiles of Life among the Animals* (New York: Henry Holt, 1998), 210–17, © copyright 1997, 1998 by Lee Gutkind, reprinted by arrangement with Henry Holt; "Waiting Away" (previously titled "Sidney Schwartz"), 15 (Spring 2000), and "Intimate Details," 18 (Winter 2002), in *Creative Nonfiction*; "Teeth," from *The People of Penn's Woods West* (Pittsburgh: University of Pittsburgh Press, 1984), 122–35; and "An Introduction: Becoming the Godfather" (previously titled "Becoming the Godfather of Creative Nonfiction") from *Writing Creative Nonfiction: Instruction and Insights from the Teachers of the Associated Writing Programs*, eds. Carolyn Forché and Philip Gerard (Cincinnati: Story Press, 2001), 170–80.